Simply Running

## An Inspirational and Common Sense Guide to Running

## With tips and information for runners in NE Florida

# Simply Running

## An Inspirational and Common Sense Guide to Running

**Mauricio Herreros**

**Old Mountain Press**

Published by:
Old Mountain Press, Inc.
2542 S. Edgewater Dr.
Fayetteville, NC 28303

www.oldmp.com

Photos: Collection of the author
**ISBN:** 1-884778-82-8
Library of Congress Catalog Card Number: 99-069854

**Simply Running**.

First Edition
Manufactured in the United States of America
1 2 3 4 5 6 7 8 9 10

# Notice

This book should be used as a reference guide only, not as a medical manual. The information provided here is intended to help you learn about the sport of running. The author offers his opinion and personal experience so that you may make an informed decision about your running and fitness program. This book is not written as a substitute for any professional medical or fitness advice. As always, with any fitness program please check with your doctor before participating in any exercise activity. Neither the author nor the publisher will assume responsibility for accidents or injuries that occur while engaging in any activities outlined in this book.

This book is dedicated to Lorrie, Sara and Christian who fill my life with joy and love.

… and to all the men and women who run in pursuit of a fit body, mind, and spirit.

# Contents

# Acknowledgments

In every major undertaking there is an individual who makes it possible. I want to thank Lorrie, my wife, for her invaluable help with every phase of the book. She was pivotal in the editing of each chapter dozens of times, always with a smile, and often putting my needs above hers. I want to thank my kids for allowing me to spend countless hours dedicated to this project. I could not have done it without your love and support.

I would also like to thank Mary Quesada for her genuine interest and help reviewing the book, Charlie Powell for his enthusiasm, and the hundreds of runners I have shared the roads with who have inspired me to run on.

Special thanks to my parents, Patricia and Humberto, who early on encouraged me to pursue my dreams, showed me the value of self-discipline and made running part of my life. My brothers, Rod and Gonzo, and my sister, Claudia, for their support and true friendship. My in-laws, Bruce and Ronnie, for their continuous encouragement. And, last but not least, Panchito, my grandfather and friend, who has given me the wings to fly.

# Introduction

Thanks for choosing my running book. Here you will find a common sense perspective derived from over sixteen years of running the track and the roads, a friendly approach from a "middle of the pack" runner. What follows is a story about a journey of perseverance and self-discovery that has helped me become a better person, and perhaps may inspire others as well.

Throughout the years, running has given me many benefits both physical and spiritual. Today I continue to receive from this wonderful sport. Running is a continuous self-rewarding activity. But, you must give it a chance to experience some of these great benefits. I once heard that, "You need to start looking to find what you are looking for."

Writing this book has been an enlightening experience. It started four years ago as a wild idea to share my running adventures. Since then I have logged thousands of miles and run many races. Each day and each new mile I have learned a little more about running and the diverse spectrum of people that call themselves "runners".

Living in Jacksonville, Florida since 1990, I have done most of my road running in this beautiful area. The local running scene has grown significantly in recent years, keeping up with the new fitness trend and the rapid growth of Northeast Florida. The good weather and beautiful outdoors invite people to run all year-round. Today, thousands of runners enjoy this running Mecca. Whether you are an experienced runner or considering this activity for the first time, *Simply Running* is a book full of useful tips and information for runners of any level. Because I started like you and learned by trial and error, this book offers valuable practical advice that can make your running experience much more enjoyable and long lasting.

*Simply Running* is intended for runners of any age and ability, and for anyone wanting to know more about this great activity. Now it is your turn to reap the benefits.

# Part One: *First Steps*

---

"A man will be remembered by his actions, not by his intentions."

# Chapter 1 - How I Started

From early in life we are greatly influenced by the people, the places, and the events around us. We are definitely shaped by these experiences, but regardless, we are usually free to take control of our destiny and become what we want to become.

The world is full of opportunities for all. With a clear goal in mind, a little determination and patience, we can go as far as we are willing to go. The limit is up to us.

## A Runner's Paradise

Whether you are a beginner or an experienced runner, Northeast Florida offers almost perfect conditions for running. The First Coast's warm spring like weather, the natural beauty of its shaded trails and scenic roads, the St. Johns River and the Intracoastal Waterway, and the long coastline with its wide clean beaches, make this area the perfect place for year-round running.

The First Coast is booming. Everywhere you look there is construction going on, new buildings, new houses, and new roads. Home to over a million people, this is one of the fastest growing areas in Florida. Thousands of people move in every month attracted by the strong economy, the low cost of living, and the prospects of a better quality of life. Keeping up with the area's healthy growth, the running community continues to expand attracting people of all ages and fitness conditions. Today, thousands of runners of all levels take advantage of the ideal running conditions of Northeast Florida. Jacksonville, the largest city in the area attracts over 8,000 runners every year to the 15K River Run. It is now common to see people running at most times of the day. After running for a while you may start to see familiar faces including celebrity runners such as American marathon record holder Jerry Lawson, upcoming Olympic star Kim Pawelek or any of the other elite runners that live and train in the area. Road races are held every weekend throughout the First Coast. Sometimes several are held the same day giving runners more options. But, if racing is not your choice there are many other alternatives like running the challenging downtown Jacksonville bridges, or through the historic center of St. Augustine, or just cruising along one of the many parks. If you are interested in the social aspect of running, the First Coast has several clubs and groups of runners open for anyone who wants to join them. No matter what your running interest is, Northeast Florida probably has something to suit your running needs.

**My Story**

We are very fortunate to live in this beautiful region of Florida where running is so easy with no freezing cold temperatures or snow to worry about. But like many people in the First Coast I'm not originally from here. We moved to Jacksonville in the spring of 1990 from New Jersey. We had been looking to transfer out of the Northeast in search of a better quality of life to raise our young family. We chose Jacksonville after visiting a few times. From the beginning we liked the natural beauty of this area, the spacious design of the city, the fact that half of everything is relatively new, and the easiness to move around. You can be in downtown in a few minutes and find parking or go to a well-maintained beach with warm water, lots of room and no entrance fee.

Like running, the First Coast grows on you. We even left Jacksonville for an overseas assignment but after ten months away decided to come back. We really missed the First Coast. After more than nine years in Northeast Florida we have become very attached to this region. It would be very difficult for us to find a better place to raise our family with so many good things available. In the beginning we thought that living here was like a well-kept

13

secret. Now with large numbers of people moving into the area we hope that the good things will remain. I guess we all can do our share to keep the First Coast a nice place for our children and ourselves.

I started road running in early 1993. Running was not completely new to me. I had done nine years of track and field competition during my youth. I was born in 1963 and grew up in Santiago, Chile, the long and narrow country in western South America. Although I graduated from college in the United States, I attended grammar school, high school, and three years of university in Chile. My dad introduced me to running early on. In January of 1972, at age 8, Dad enrolled me in a year-round track and field program at "Stadio Italiano", a large sports club in Santiago. I trained and competed for this club until 1980. Sport clubs are common in Chile. In Santiago alone there are several well-established clubs that were started by different groups of immigrants during the first half of the century. Some of them are the French club, the German club, the Spanish club, the Croatian club, the Jewish club, the Palestinian club, the Syrian club, the English club, and the Italian club I trained at among several others.

In the beginning we had track practice three times per week. Each practice lasted over an hour. Practice consisted of a warm up jog followed by a few minutes of stretching. Then we worked on speed doing a series of short intervals. After this each kid worked on technique for his/ her field event. Practice always ended with a cool down exercise. We had two excellent coaches. They worked with each kid closely. My specialties were the long jump and sprint events. The track was well kept. The grass turf was good for training, but not fast enough for racing. It wasn't the best place to set a personal record. Years later the club invested in a clay turf, which was the best at that time. I liked the clay turf, because it was faster and smoother. The spikes of my racing shoes sank in the track much better.

On September 11, 1973, an event that changed the history of Chile and surprised most of the world took place. A coup was carried out by the armed forces. The leftist government and president were overthrown. Warplanes bombed and destroyed the 150-year-old presidential palace. Tanks blockaded the downtown district. The

Navy closed the main ports. Every town was put under military control. The nation had been on the verge of civil war. The military established a strict curfew and martial law that lasted for months. Many people died during the weeks after the coup. It was a difficult time for Chile and a high price to pay for progress. Schools were closed for several weeks before and after the coup. People had become suspicious of each other. Food and most goods were scarce. The country was paralyzed by the turmoil. My parents had stopped taking me to track practice because it was too dangerous to venture out on the streets. During the days of the coup we had to avoid the front windows of our house for fear of stray bullets. One morning we found a bullet that had broken my father's pick-up truck windshield. After a few more weeks things began to return to normal. Schools reopened and I went back to the track.

As the years went by I became more involved with my track training. I was competing at club and school tournaments. This type of competition required me to go to practice 4 days per week. This was a lot since I was still responsible for my schoolwork and household chores. Being the oldest of four children didn't help much since I was always expected to set the example for my brothers and sister. One year while competing at the National Stadium, I won the 400 meters 11-12 year old boys' race. To my surprise a few days later, a picture of me winning this race appeared on the cover of the country's largest newspaper. This picture became part of the logo for a brand of Nestle kids' cereal. A couple of years before another picture had been taken of me winning the 400 meters at a track club tournament. That picture appeared in newspapers and a well-known sports commentator made references to it on TV to promote youth sports. These two events were my only experiences of national fame during my track career.

We first came to the United States in July 1975. My parents, my sister and I toured Florida, and visited relatives in New York and Minneapolis. I was impressed by the United States and wished to return someday. Back in Chile, I continued to train intensively focusing mainly on the long jump. I worked hard to improve my jumping technique and speed. At some practices I had to do speed intervals around the track dragging an old truck tire tied with a rope around my waist. Later, I felt light as a feather running without the extra weight.

I have always been a little restless with lots of energy and desire to try new things. This is probably why in 1977 I joined a karate school. Mom had attended the school for a month and I got interested in the idea of self-defense. I was still doing track four times per week so balancing both sports and high school became an art. Somehow I managed to practice karate for the next two years. This is how martial arts became my second sport. I admired the oriental philosophy and mental discipline. In 1978, I qualified for the national track championship held at Santiago's National Stadium. Between 4-8 kids were chosen to represent each region of the country in each track and field event. I was representing Santiago, a city of 4 million. The stadium's track turf had been replaced with the latest artificial material. Only three stadiums in Chile had this new type of turf. It was harder and more bouncy. I felt proud to be running on the latest technology available. We had to use special short spikes with flat heads to avoid damaging the synthetic turf. I competed in the long jump and finished in 5th place. This was very good nationally, but I was disappointed because I couldn't get a medal. All my family had come to see me at the stadium. By the end of this year at age 15, I was ranked among the top ten long jumpers for my age group in the country. I was jumping over 21 feet and running the 100 meters in 12 seconds flat. In late 1979, I started to lose interest in running perhaps due to the type of commitment required to go to the next level. I was still running but needed to train six days per week to remain among the top competitors. After almost nine continuos years, I felt burned out and my motivations were changing. Now almost a senior in high school, I wanted to spend more time with my friends, and had to prepare for college, which was right around the corner.

In 1980, I decreased my training significantly. By the end of that year I was no longer running. Dad wasn't very happy, but he didn't give me much grief. Years later some of my running mates that kept going became nationally known and got scholarships to train and study in Europe and the United States. A few went to the Olympic games in 1984, 1988, and 1992. Perhaps I missed a good chance for competing internationally. I'll never know. But, I don't regret it much because I experienced other aspects of life, which I would have missed otherwise. In June 1980 during my senior year winter break, I traveled alone to the United States to visit my relatives in New York. I had chosen this trip instead of the high school class trip to Brazil a year earlier. I spent a month in New York City and Washington DC. At first, our cultures seemed similar but later I found subtle differences. In America, young people wanted to move out of their parents' home when they turned 18. In Chile young people stayed with their parents until they got married, which could be well into their 20s. In a way, I admired the early independence of Americans, perhaps because I was always more independent myself. I was very impressed with the quality of things in the United States. Everything seemed functional and working properly. Although, Chile had lots of unused land, the cities seemed smaller and congested. I liked the spaciousness of the US cities and how easily accessible everything was. By the time I had to go back, I had decided to return someday to study in college.

I graduated from high school in December 1980. Soon after, I left for college spending the first half of 1981 in Viña del Mar, a coastal city in central Chile. This was my first time away from home and I missed it. During my first year of college I had stopped both running and Karate. I was too busy with school. I returned home in 1981 and was accepted at a local university in Santiago. In 1982, I started running again, this time for my college's track team at "Universidad de Santiago". I qualified for the long jump event. I trained for three months preparing for the tournament season, but had to quit because of a painful injury to both heels. It felt like a small stress fracture. This put an end to my short college track career. I never returned to the track after the injury. Feeling in need of exercise, a few months later I started martial arts again. This time I practiced Kung Fu for one year. In 1983, at age 19, I signed up in a voluntary ROTC program with the Chilean Army. I had always admired the military career. The order, discipline, clear goals, and adventure of military life interested me. I chose an all-terrain motorcycle brigade, a special unit of the armored division of the army. I was a sophomore in college and had a full load of engineering courses. The army required that I participate in military training every Saturday, with one weekend activity per month and two weeks of military exercises per year. The objective was that in two years I would become a second lieutenant of the army reserve forces. Each soldier had access to a new all-terrain motorcycle. It was exciting. The time was divided into lecture and practical exercises. One night, the exercise involved walking all night on nearby hills. We each carried a weapon and a fully loaded backpack. Our mission was to reach the other side of a mountain without being caught by enemy forces. I remember getting lost from my platoon in the smoke and confusion caused by a mortar attack. I stayed down on the ground for a few minutes, which seemed like hours. It was very dark and I thought my unit was hiding as well. After not seeing anyone else I realized that they had left me behind. I crawled up the hill to avoid being detected and captured. A few minutes later, I heard friendly voices on the other side. From the top of the hill I saw my platoon waiting at the bottom of the hill. I ran down a few hundred yards to join them. A sergeant was waiting for me. He shouted at me for staying behind. The walk back to the base took two hours. Military training was tough. This was the real stuff. It had taken me a few weeks to realize this truth. I used to come home worn out and bruised. Mom didn't like it, but I enjoyed being part of this group of would-be soldiers. Our captain was a tough guy, a career officer. He was very proud of his military life and inspired a lot of respect and admiration from us.

In March 1984, I accepted the offer from an American friend to study in the United States. His father was working for a mining company in Chile. He came to visit during the summers. Our parents agreed that I would live with them in Tucson and would transfer my computer science courses to the University of Arizona. I was excited. My wishes were materializing. I began preparing myself to leave Chile in August of that year. Mom and I convinced Dad to let me try this adventure. He was worried that I would lose my three years of college in Chile. Just in case, I requested a year leave of absence from the university to keep a door open if things didn't go well in Arizona. I asked for my dismissal from the ROTC program because I was traveling to the United States. Both requests were approved. I sold my small car to save the money for college. At last I had a green light to proceed with the trip. During the weeks before my departure, I was worried about leaving my family and friends, but decided to carry out the original plan. I left Chile on August 8, 1984. That day my life took a big turn. Upon my arrival in the United States, I spent the first two weeks at my uncle's farm in Gainesville, Florida. Little I did know that I would settle down in northeast Florida years later. I had arrived here to meet my grandfather and drive together to New York City.

My main reason for being in the States was to enroll in the University of Arizona as a transfer student. When we arrived in New York, I decided to get a temporary job that would help me save money for school. After all, school wouldn't start until January. Basically, I had four months to work and stay with my relatives in New York. I liked the idea of working because it would help me improve my English faster than attending a class. Surprisingly in October 1984, I found a temporary job at the United Nations. This job kept me in New York longer than originally planned. I rented a studio in Queens for a year. I joined the local YMCA to attend a Karate class twice per week. I hadn't exercised much in two years, so it felt good to get back in shape. I began jogging a little but very infrequently. The United Nations was a fascinating place to work. My job was with the conference services department, so I met many famous diplomats and politicians from all over the world. People from every country in the world worked at the UN. There were six official languages, but with so many foreigners, the UN seemed like the tower of Babel. My experience there was very valuable and eye opening.

In April 1985, at a UN work party, I met the most beautiful girl of my life. She was from New Jersey and had been working in the United Nations guided tours department. I had walked by her desk many times, but we hadn't seen each other. It was love at first sight. After the party, we started dating and spent most of our free time together. She quickly became my guide to American culture and helped me tremendously to keep moving forward. Since she was an English major it was like having my own private teacher. I learned more English with her than in all the courses I'd taken before. Later that summer, I ran my first long distance race in the United States, a 1-mile run at the United Nations Park. I finished among the first 10 runners in 5:35 minutes. I was exhausted from the effort and the lack of adequate training. In September my work contract was extended another year. In 1986, I moved to New Jersey to be closer to my fiancee and because the commute to New York City was shorter. During this time, I had been taking computer courses at a New York City college. I was not happy attending school part-time because it was taking longer than expected. Around this time, the US Army offered me to enroll in a 6-year enlistment program in exchange for a full GI Bill scholarship to pay for college. I seriously considered their offer and even took the Armed Forces' ASVAB tests. At the last minute, I changed my mind after receiving an acceptance letter from Rutgers University as a transfer student. All my previous college courses had been validated towards the computer science major. Now, I was only four semesters away from getting my bachelor degree. By this time I was running very infrequently. I was no longer going to the YMCA. In the spring of 1986, I ran the 1-mile race for the 40th anniversary celebration of the United Nations. I lowered my time to 5:30 minutes but felt extremely out of shape.

In September of 1986, Lorrie and I got married at the New York City Hall. We didn't tell our families until a day later. It was a happy surprise for everyone. We agreed to have a private religious ceremony a month later. My wife's parents planned a big wedding reception after the church ceremony. At the time my father-in-law was the mayor of the town they lived in, in Union County, New Jersey. He owned a restaurant/ bakery that had been in the family for fifty years. Their apple pies and cider were famous in the area. I had married the beautiful daughter of a very traditional and upbeat American family. My parents and sister came from Chile to attend the religious ceremony and wedding reception. We were both a little nervous having our parents meet for the first time, but everything went smoothly and we all had a wonderful time together. A few months later, I quit my job at the UN and enrolled full time at Rutgers University. During 1987, I had little time for fitness since I put all my focus on school. It was now or never for my degree. In December 1987, I graduated with a degree in computer science. I was happy that school was over.

Lorrie and I enjoyed seeing new places so we got in the habit of driving from town to town through the Northeastern States. We did this during weekends and mini vacations. After my graduation we spent seven weeks in Chile visiting family and traveling. When we got back to the States, I was offered a job as computer programmer with the telephone company in New Jersey. During this time, I was not active in sports except for a few runs on the high school track and riding my bike. Although, I have always been very independent and a bit of a loner, I keep very close ties with my parents and siblings. In 1988, my wife and I invited my two younger brothers to move in with us, so that they could attend high school in the States. We knew that this would be a big responsibility both financially and emotionally, but I wanted them to have the experience of living in the United States from an early age. I wanted them to learn English and develop their full potential in school and in sports. Upon arrival, both were selected to join the varsity soccer team. They played soccer through their remaining high school and college years. In 1989, our beautiful daughter was born. By now, my time was spent with the baby, family, brothers, and work. Fitness was not much in my mind, although, I could've benefited from it.

As I mentioned before in March 1990, I accepted a transfer opportunity to Jacksonville, Florida. Two months later in the late spring we arrived in the First Coast. By now I really wanted to get back in shape. I was feeling extra tired and had put on a few excess pounds. Five months later I joined a Taekwondo school in Jacksonville. It felt great to be exercising again. I practiced this martial arts style for the next several years. That summer an opportunity came up at work to enroll in an MBA weekend program. I took it. In September I found myself attending college again. The addition of schoolwork to my regular responsibilities kept me very busy for the next two years. I still managed to attend Taekwondo class twice per week. I completed the MBA program in July 1992. This time I was really glad it was over. Ironically I never made it to Tucson. By now my friend had married and was working in Phoenix. Life has many surprises.

In the spring of 1993, I was feeling unchallenged and bored with martial arts. I found myself thinking of reasons to skip class. It didn't make sense since I was paying $50 per month. This was my third year of Taekwondo. At 29 years of age, I had started to gain extra weight around my waist. The twice a week Taekwondo workout was not enough to keep me in good shape. The combination of my diet and sedentary computer programmer job compounded the problem. My challenge was to find a sport that I could blend with my family life, work, and Taekwondo schedule since I wasn't ready to throw away years of martial arts practice. At the time my wife was attending an aerobics class. I thought of trying this activity, but it wasn't easy to find classes open for both men and women. The reality was that most men didn't do aerobics. I needed a practical and convenient sport. I remembered my earlier years of track and decided to start running again. Running seemed the perfect choice. Although, I was never a long distance runner, I thought my years of track and martial arts training would make running easy for me. The first step was to get a pair of running shoes. I asked a friend at work and he recommended the "Pegasus". In April 1993, I bought my first pair of NIKE Air Pegasus®. That same evening I measured a loop around my house of about 2 miles and went out on my first "real" run since 1986. After running a few blocks, I had pain in both legs and a stitch in my side. It didn't make sense since I considered myself able to run a few blocks. I barely completed that first run. Later that night, I realized that my running muscles had not been used in a long time and that the martial arts training had not developed my aerobic capacity. This little discovery motivated me to start training on a regular basis to redevelop my running condition. My youngest brother Gonzo, who was still living with us, started running with me in the evenings. At 21, he was in good shape from playing soccer. From the beginning he ran faster and longer than me. My goal was to beat him or at least keep up with him.

Running had returned to my rescue, completing a full circle to where I had left it twelve years earlier. After a month of running, my motivation was growing stronger. I continued to lose interest in the martial arts classes. What kept me going was that I had a year contract with the school. Some days I ran, others I attended Taekwondo class. It was a struggle, but I felt that at least I was benefiting from the cross-training aspect. In July, my brother and I ran our first race in Florida. It was great. That evening I didn't win a medal, but I got hooked on running. I now wanted to discover the whole new world of road running that was unfolding before my eyes. That same month, my wonderful son was born in Jacksonville. Now with two small kids I really needed to keep training to stay in shape for my family. For the remaining part of the 1993 I continued to run two or three times per week. In February 1994, I was transferred to Chile for a year. We sold our house and moved in the spring. At first, I was very happy to be back home after a decade in the United States. I started training on weekends at the old track club. My work in Chile was very demanding and left me with little time for sports. After ten stressful months we decided to return to Jacksonville at the end of 1994. We were glad to be back. We missed the clean air, the spaciousness, the beautiful beaches and the St. Johns River. Jacksonville was the best place to raise our family. I was anxious to start running again. Running in Florida was a lot easier than in Chile. In Jacksonville, I had more time, the traffic was less of a threat, and there were no unsupervised dogs chasing me away. I established a running routine of four days per week averaging a total of 20 miles or less. I became one of the guys you see running on the streets of Northeast Florida.

Since 1993 I have never stopped running the roads. I have completed dozens of road races including five 15K River Runs, many 5K, 5M, 10K, half marathons, and a marathon. Although I have had some injuries and low periods, my running has endured despite all the obstacles. Overall, I have run several thousand miles and worn out many pairs of running shoes. Four years ago, we moved to St. John's County where I do most of my weekly runs. My training routine has settled into 4 runs per week with a combination of stretching, and upper body exercises. This helps me maintain a more balanced fitness. I have finally motivated my wife to start running. She has been doing it steadily for over a year. Our kids have started to appreciate sports and have participated in several fun runs. Running has become an important part of my lifestyle, but more importantly of our family life. Today, I see myself running many years from now, a sort of lifetime runner.

What is your story? Have you ever thought how you got this far?

60 meters final, school track & field championship, Santiago, Chile (1975). Author in top lane.

With teammates at track club in Chile (1977). Author second from left.

1 mile race. United Nations, New York (1985).

# Chapter 2 - To Run or Not to Run

Since the end of the last century people have become very sedentary. Many of us have office jobs, which require us to sit in front of a computer or desk for hours every day. It seems that as the world becomes more technologically advanced we do less physical work, and our bodies become more and more idle. This is not good for our long term well being since the human body was designed to be active. Physical activity is a basic human need. It is our natural state of being. Without regular exercise our body begins to deteriorate at a much faster rate. Running regularly, two or three times per week, can improve our overall health. It can jump-start our sedentary lifestyles.

In the last two decades hundreds of scientific studies have confirmed the positive side effects of a moderate exercise routine in adults. Further research has shown that running can help reduce stress, lower high blood pressure, alleviate arthritis, and lower the risks of some types of cancer, and osteoporosis in women. This is no news to me since I have been running for many years and feeling healthy and strong. Running is a great exercise. In fact it is one of the most effective and complete exercise activities we know of.

**20 Good Reasons to Run**

This is a starting point. Think of what additional benefits you have found in your running experience.
- It is easy to learn. You can start at your own pace by combining walking and running.

- It will help you stay in good physical shape. You will become an ambassador of fitness, inspiring those around you.
- It will help you lose excess weight. Exercise is a better and healthier choice than dieting.
- It can help you keep the doctor away when overall health is improved with regular exercise (at least three times per week 30 minutes each).
- It is one of the best activities to improve cardiovascular fitness. Runners usually have a lower number of heartbeats per minute than non-runners during rest time.
- It will help you maintain a good mental attitude and a positive outlook on life.
- It will help you reduce stress in your life and become a more relaxed person.
- It makes you feel good because you are doing something for yourself. It is an invigorating and energizing experience. Completing each run is an accomplishment.
- It will help you discover your true potential. You will get to know yourself better.
- It is a convenient form of exercise. You can run anytime and anywhere, and in most areas of the country you can run year round.
- Running is a high aerobic sport, but its flexibility allows you to set attainable goals tailored to your desires and limitations.
- It is a relatively low cost activity. All you need are a good pair of running shoes and running clothes. There are no club fees.
- If you want challenge, running can be it when you set higher goals and measure progress against own performance.
- If you want solitude, you can run alone and use your daily runs to mediate.
- If you want competition, races provide the excitement you need. You will feel like a world-class runner at the long distance events. Races are optional for a small fee.
- If you are a social person, you can run with friends or join a running club. At races you can meet nice people with similar interests and make long lasting friendships.
- It is a family activity. You can run with your partner, kids, friends, or dog. It allows you to be creative.

- It is one of the few sports where you can mix with world-class athletes. At races throughout the country you can meet and run with some of the best long distance runners in the world.
- It offers adventure and fun. Every run is different. It will take you to new places.
- It is a lifestyle, a way of life, a long term activity.

Are there any disadvantages to running? As with everything there are exceptions to the general rule. Extreme running can lead to injuries and burnout. As with any physical activity it is recommended that you consult a doctor prior to engaging in any regular exercise program or routine. I recommend that runners get an annual health checkup as a preventive and common sense measure.

Have I convinced you? Exercise is good. Running is cool. There is only one way to find out. You owe it to yourself to discover how running can benefit you. Are you still undecided? Go watch a local road race in your area. They are usually held on Saturday mornings. Observe the enthusiasm and camaraderie shared by runners. I believe you will be pleasantly surprised and it may motivate you to start running. Who knows, perhaps in the near future you will be running in one of them too.

**Why I Run**

"A layer of sweat covers my face, neck, and back. I am past the half point of the 4-mile run. My breathing is deep and steady. I feel the tension in my muscles as my thighs, calves, and shoulders work harmoniously in every stride. For a few moments, I imagine myself floating, just barely touching the pavement in a perfect rhythm of moving forces. Different thoughts come and go. I am just enjoying the moment. A car is coming. I move off the road. I don't want to take any chances. The morning is sunny and humid. A mild breeze cools my face. The temperature is in the 60s and rising, another beautiful spring day in Jacksonville. The car passes by. I am back on the road. I check my watch. My pace is now even at 8 minutes per mile. I feel the energy flowing through my body like wind blowing through a storm. I make the familiar turn. I know now in a few minutes I'll be home. I pick up my stride. I want to finish strong. It is great to be alive and great to be running".

What makes me run? What keeps me going day after day? What are my motivations for getting out there in the cold, rain, or hot sun, to do my scheduled run? Why do I feel so happy the morning of a race, knowing that I have little chance of winning? How long will I keep doing this? Will I ever stop running? Perhaps, like most runners, I have asked myself these questions many times. The answers are not easily available. We must look inside. I believe that by seeking answers to these questions, we will discover important clues about ourselves.

When I started running the roads, my main motivations were to maintain good health, to lose weight and to get back in shape. I wanted an activity that didn't require me to pay a monthly fee or to join a gym. I needed convenience. I wanted freedom. Running was fun and satisfied my initial needs. After my first race, I was hooked. I enjoyed the feeling of competition against others and myself. It reminded me of the high school track years when winning was one of my main goals. I loved the warm feeling of running a good race and setting a personal record. Being at road races made me feel young, powerful, and full of energy. At the starting line, I stood in the first row with the fastest runners, feeling like a world class athlete. Putting on my race clothes and running shoes became a special ritual, almost a sacred one. Running empowered me, and I became addicted to this feeling. During this time, my running was focused mainly towards road racing. I knew that hard training would prepare me better for the next race, so I motivated myself to run on hot, rainy, and cold days. I enjoyed adding challenges to my training since these would make me a stronger runner. In a period of two years, I ran forty races including a marathon. This was a time of great personal satisfaction. I proved to myself that with training, I could consistently improve my race times, and that I was in better shape than in the previous ten years.

During my third year of running, I felt burned out from racing and started to get injuries more frequently. I reevaluated my goals and decided to cut back my training and racing. I even tried to quit for a while but couldn't. I knew that inside me there were some powerful reasons that kept me running. I began to look for the real motives that kept me going. While searching for answers, I started noticing that a positive transformation was taking place within me. For the first time, I saw myself, less perfect than I wished to admit, but more human and wanting to learn. Running awakened me from a long sleep, from a dream where money and material goals were above people and spiritual growth. Running helped me see things differently. My priorities were slowly shifting. It became clearer what I wanted in my life. I started to appreciate the people and things in my life I had usually taken for granted. I began a process of self-discovery. I realized that running was not just about winning races and awards. Instead, it offered me much more. I saw running as a journey, and a unique opportunity to grow spiritually. It represented a new way of life. Running opened up a window to my inner self. Through this connection I became more aware of who I am and my purpose in this life. I discovered that the journey is as important as the destination, and that we must find the balance between working towards our goals and enjoying what we already have. Because I am a competitive person I still enjoyed running races and winning, but now, I treasured the unique experience of every run. I realized that each run is a gift, a special moment to learn more about oneself and to experience the greatness of life.

Today, I continue to run for these reasons and more. Above all, I do it because I enjoy it. It helps me stay fit and feel healthy. When I'm out running my worries seem to disappear. I feel free and more alive. I wake up happier in the morning and sleep better at night. Running gives me inner peace. In my solitary runs I feel my body, mind, and spirit together as one form. Running is self-rewarding and spiritually enriching. I feel the presence of God and surrounding nature more close and real. Sometimes during my runs I feel like an explorer. I get to see different places and meet interesting people. It is an adventure. Running has helped me set a good example for my children and family. Now we all like to run. It is a great family activity and it keeps us more united. Running is a challenge, and every time I do it, I feel good about myself. Especially, when I am tired after a long day of work, or when it is freezing cold, or raining hard, or hot and humid, but I put on my running gear and go out anyway. The simple accomplishment of completing each run gives me the pride, confidence and energy to keep coming back for more. I believe that when we run we are making a positive statement to the world. We are leading the way for others, overcoming obstacles, one mile at a time. In a way we represent the power and determination of the human spirit. Ultimately, running helps us bring out our true potential as athletes and as human beings.

Sometime ago, I thought what running meant to me.

> "Whether it rains or shines,
> whether it is cold or warm,
> whether it is early or late,
> I go out for my solitary run.
>
> Running is my hideout from the world,
> it is where I relieve the stress of the day,
> where I feel my breathing and can taste my sweat,
> where my body, mind, and soul reunite,
> it is the place where thoughts come and go,
> where I find myself alone, just me and the road,
> where problems don't matter anymore,
> it is the place where I feel safer and closer to God,
> where I feel younger, full of energy and life.
>
> Running is my refuge."

# Chapter 3 - Running Gear

One of the great advantages of running is that it requires very little equipment. Basically, all you need are running shoes and some running clothes.

## Shoes

Perhaps the most important item for a runner is his running shoes. This makes sense since while protecting our feet, running shoes help reduce the shock the body receives as we hit the road with each stride. An old worn pair of shoes, however, can significantly diminish overall performance as well as increase the risk of running injuries. I guess you get the point. If you want to enjoy a long injury-free running experience don't neglect the condition of your running shoes.

Thanks to technology in recent years there have been tremendous improvements in the quality of running shoes. Twenty years ago the quality was significantly worse. The top running shoes of the 1970's would be many times more deficient than the basic running shoes of today. Looking back at the first pair of spike shoes I owned in 1972, I am amazed that I was able to run in them and not get serious injuries. They had a wooden sole with no cushioning!

Today, we can choose from a wide variety of excellent running shoes available on the market. In fact there are so many different models, styles, and prices that it can be an overwhelming task to try to find the right model. One way to narrow down the selection is to learn a little about your foot type since running shoes are built primarily with this factor in mind.

## Foot Types

This information will help you and the sales person identify the best model for your unique needs. Basically, there are three distinct categories of foot type. In reality most people fall somewhere in between two types, but it helps to get an idea of which classification we are closest to. There is a simple test that you can do to determine your foot type. It is called the wet test and I will describe it in detail in this section. Keep in mind that when in doubt you can always go to a specialty running store. They should have experienced sales people that can help you identify your exact foot type and the shoes that best meet your particular bio-mechanical needs.

The wet test is simple and consists of the following:

1. Wet your bare foot and make a footprint on a flat, dry surface. (i.e. driveway). Don't strike the ground too hard. Pretend that you are walking normally.

2. Observe the footprint and try to match it with one of the following descriptions:

- If your footprint is very full and shows no arch, in other words the print shows your entire foot and it is wide, you probably have a <u>flat foot</u> with low arch.
- If your footprint shows the entire foot with a moderate curve where the arch rises off the ground, you most likely have a <u>normal foot</u> with normal arch.
- If your footprint shows mainly the ball and the heel of your foot, in other words the print is curved and very little of the middle of your foot is shown, you probably have a <u>high arched</u> foot.

3. Based on the type of footprint identified in the preceding step we can determine the degree of pronation of your feet. Pronation is the natural rotation of the foot inward and downward when we

hit the ground. This motion helps the foot absorb the shock of impact.

- A <u>low arched or flat foot</u> indicates that you have a tendency to overpronate. In other words the foot rolls too far inward when you strike the ground. This is a common problem and can lead to lower leg injuries if you run with the wrong type of shoes.
- A <u>normal arched or normal foot</u> indicates that you are probably a normal pronator. This means that as your foot strikes the ground you roll inward normally absorbing the shock of the impact well. In other words your feet are bio-mechanically efficient when hitting the ground.
- A <u>high arched foot</u> indicates that you probably are an underpronator. This means that your foot doesn't roll inward enough when you strike the ground. In other words your feet don't absorb shock well.

The good news is that no matter what type of foot you have, the shoe companies have developed running shoes for almost every foot type and bio-mechanical need.

**Types of Running Shoes**

Running shoes come mainly in one of three shapes: straight, semi-curved, and curved. Each shape offers advantages to at least one of the three foot types described earlier. Keep in mind that this is not an absolute rule and runners will have personal preferences as to what type of shoe shape "feels" better to them.

- The runner with flat feet or low arch should try straight or semi-curved shape shoes. Since people with flat feet tend to overpronate, the shoes selected should reduce the degree of pronation.

- The runner with normal feet or normal pronation and not overweight will find that semi-curved shape shoes suit him/her best.

- The runner with high-arched feet is most likely an underpronator and should try the curved shape shoes. The running shoes selected should encourage foot motion while allowing flexibility.

Running shoes can further be classified into the following categories according to the expected use and built-in features: motion control, stability, cushioned, lightweight training, cross-country trail, and racing.

Once you know your foot type and have decided the shape of shoes you want, you need to think about where you will be doing most of the running with these shoes. In other words what type of surface do you plan to run on most often (i.e. road asphalt, beach, dirt, grass, trail, track)? Shoes wear out differently depending on the surface they are most used on. For example, if you know that you will be running mainly on asphalt you should consider more cushioned shoes than if you were to do your runs on grass.

The following is a brief description of each category of shoes:

Motion-Control Shoes

- Motion-control shoes are rigid, control-oriented shoes. These shoes are usually heavier but last longer. They are designed to reduce overpronation. They feature a strong midsole for durability. They usually have a straight shape. Runners that overpronate or have flat feet and want durability should try these shoes. Heavier runners can benefit from the extra control provided by these shoes.

Stability Shoes

- Stability shoes usually have a semi-curved shape. These shoes are excellent if you need a balance of midsole support, cushioning, and durability. If you are not overweight and have a normal arched foot, you may like these shoes.

Cushioned Shoes

- Cushioned shoes offer the softest midsole. They do not have very strong medial support. These shoes are built in a semi-curved or curved shape to allow more foot motion. These shoes are good for underpronators or runners with high arches.

## Lightweight Training Shoes

- Lightweight shoes are lighter than standard training shoes. If you are a beginning runner you don't need to spend your money on these shoes. Lightweight training shoes are a nice thing to have if you are an efficient runner and want to do speed or track work. Never use these as your primary training shoes. Lightweight training shoes have a semi-curved or curved shape and are less durable than standard training shoes. Some runners use these shoes for racing if they want more support and cushioning than the even lighter racing shoes.

## Cross-country Trail Shoes

- If you plan to do most of your runs on a rugged terrain or off-road trails you may want to consider these shoes. I would not use them for road running. Trail shoes are built with reinforcements around the sides and toe area for protection and durability. They have better sole traction than standard training shoes and tend to be heavier.

## Racing Shoes

- Racing shoes are light. These shoes should not be used for training since they have very little cushioning. You risk getting injuries if do your training runs in these shoes. The main purpose of these shoes is racing. This means that they are super light and will not last as long as the standard training shoes. I recommend that you only consider buying racing shoes after 6 months to one year of continuous training and after you have run a few races. The racing exposure will give you a better idea of your racing goals. Additionally, by then your commitment to running will justify the extra expense. Don't buy these shoes if you have no plans of racing.

## Buying Running Shoes

- Always try both shoes. Wear a pair of socks that you use to run. Walk around the store. Ask if you can test drive the shoes by running to the corner and back.
- Running shoes tend to run smaller than regular shoes. This means that you will probably want at least half a number larger than your regular shoes. Don't assume that you will take the same size always. Try every pair before buying. Sizes are not consistent even within the same model line. Most shoes will stretch a little with wear.
- Don't assume that the most expensive shoes with the most features are necessarily the best for you. Compare models and decide what you want in your shoes first. Try different models to gain a feeling of which shoes best meet your needs. Some running specialty stores let you buy a pair, take them home, try them and exchange them if you realize that weren't what you wanted. Ask your sales person about this option.
- A good time to buy shoes is after a workout or late in the day when your feet are most swollen.
- Keep in mind that feet swell a little during running. Also, as we age, feet will get a little bit bigger.
- Avoid lightweight shoes for training. These are designed for very efficient runners with normal arches. You can always get a pair of lighter shoes for racing or running short distances.
- Men's shoes run wider than women's. Some women with wider feet can fit better in men's shoes.
- Bring your old shoes to the running specialty store. The experienced sales clerks can identify your foot type by looking at the wear pattern.

Everyone should try to find the model and type of running shoes that best meets their needs. Of course this can take time, some luck, and a lot of trial and error experience. I have bought many pairs of shoes since I started running. In the past I made mistakes buying the lower priced models to realize later that the shoes weren't what I needed. On the other hand the most expensive shoes may not be the best either. With these sometimes you are paying for the bells and whistles that most people don't need. Perhaps the best advice I can give you is to try several models and ask lots of questions. If price is not a concern you have a lot of good choices.

If you don't want to spend too much money look around for specials. When a specific model is discontinued, stores lower the price to make room for the new models. This way I have saved 20-30% on some very nice models that I wanted. In many years of running I have accumulated several pairs of shoes. I keep two good pairs for training plus at least one older pair for backup including running in the rain or beach. I keep a few retired running shoes for leisure activities. For racing I bought a lightweight pair. I only use it for races. These shoes are very soft and flexible. The first time I wore them I was running a 5K race. I felt so light that almost could not tell if I had shoes on. I was flying. Part of the trade-off with racing shoes is that they have less cushioning support. Since most of my races are middle distances between 5K and 15K, these shoes are okay. I would not recommend running a marathon with them since they don't have enough cushioning for such a distance. When I ran the 1996 New York Marathon, I wore a medium weight pair, which was lighter than the regular trainers but provided enough cushioning for the 26.2 miles of road pounding.

When shopping for running shoes keep in mind that your needs are different from everyone else's and that there is a model out there just for you. Once you find the right model, consider getting two pairs right away since models can change drastically from year to year. This way you will ensure that you have another good pair waiting for you when the first one is worn out. Things can change fast in today's world and running shoes are no exception. But don't despair. There will always be plenty of running shoes to choose from. They may just be different models to get used to. To get the latest models and reviews check the Runners' World web site. They publish a spring and fall running shoe review every year (www.runnersworld.com).

**Tracking the Miles**

So you bought your first pair of running shoes. Congratulations! You have made a big step towards a joyful life as a runner. It is a good habit to track the miles of your shoes so that you know when it is time to replace them. This will help you prevent injuries caused by worn out shoes. Experts estimate the life of a standard pair of running shoes at anywhere from 350 to 500 miles. The exact number of miles will ultimately depend on the runner's weight and type of foot. Personally, I average between 450 to 550 miles on my shoes. When they get past 550 miles, I know it is time to retire them to low-impact activities such as walking or just leisure.

But why only 400, 450, or 500 miles per pair of shoes? It is important to understand what happens to the shoes as we run with them. Running shoes wear out mainly on the sole and the inside cushioning. As the cushioning thins out we are more exposed to injuries. During a run, feet hit the ground thousands of times. It has been estimated that the feet of an average runner will touch the ground about 1600 times per mile. So, in a 5K run (3.1 miles) a runner will make almost 5000 strides, hitting the ground each time. Over time this can turn into hundreds of thousands and perhaps millions of strides pounding the ground with our shoes and feet. At the above rate, it would take about 650 miles to complete one million strides. Then 450 miles per shoes doesn't seem too conservative anymore. Studies show that 25% of the shock absorption of running shoes is lost after 50 miles, 33% is lost after 150 miles, and 40% is lost after 300 miles or more.

The best way to accurately know the number of miles on a pair of running shoes is to track the miles you have run on them. This is where the *running log* comes into place. In addition to providing a place to record your training and racing events, the running log allows you to monitor the accumulated mileage of your running shoes. This will help you prevent injuries. Without a running log it becomes very difficult to keep an accurate record of the miles completed with each pair of running shoes. You may think that tracking the miles on each pair of shoes takes away the freedom of running. Believe me, I agree with you. At first it seems a waste of time, but soon after, you will get used to keeping a record of your running activities. It gives me peace of mind to know that at any time I can quickly figure out the usage on a pair of shoes.

Many overuse injuries start with a worn out pair of running shoes. The running log will help you know when a pair is ready for retirement. As I stated before, I usually keep two or three active pairs of running shoes for my training. I keep a separate pair for races, which I never train in. I originally assigned label numbers to all my running shoes (i.e. A1, A2, A3, …A8). I used the first letter of the shoe brand and a unique number. When I buy a new pair I use the next label number available and add it to my running log. Every time I run, I note the approximate mileage along with the label number for the shoes I wore for the run. On a regular basis, I add up all the miles for each pair of shoes. This is a convenient way to monitor their usage. In addition, the running log gives me a quick picture of the number of miles I am doing per week or month. Although not needed for tracking the shoes mileage, I record the times of my runs, and other information such as location of the run, terrain, time of day, weather, how I felt, etc. You can customize the log to include your own preferences of information. There are several software packages available for runners, which include different versions of running logs. I created my own log using Microsoft Excel®. For those that don't want to bother with PCs there are several versions of paper logs that you can buy at most running stores or bookstores. The nice thing about a paper running log is that you can take with you everywhere unlike the PC version.

One last tip, avoid wearing your active running shoes for leisure activities or other sports since you won't be tracking the extra usage and it does add up over time. Shoes may still look good on the outside while the inside cushioning could be seriously worn out.

**Maintaining your Shoes**

Running shoes are expensive. They can easily cost in the range of $70 - $130 per pair of shoes, and as you learned in the preceding section they won't last forever. Most likely shoes will last about six months for a runner averaging 20 miles per week. Therefore it is smart to protect your investment by applying a few common sense tips that will ensure that the shoes remain in good condition during their expected lifetime.

Store your shoes in a dry place and keep them away from the sun. I built a three-level shelf where I keep all my running shoes. I keep them in my bedroom closet, but they could be kept anywhere in the house as long as they are not exposed to constant humidity or heat. If they get wet or muddy try to clean them as soon as possible with a dampened rag or paper towel, then place them in a dry area away from direct exposure to the sun. Avoid wetting the shoes completely since it could affect the cushioning materials inside the shoe. Never put the shoes in the dryer as this can seriously damage the shoe fiber materials as well as your machine. A few months ago while running in the rain my 1-month old pair of shoes got very wet and after they dried they felt much tighter in the upper part of the shoe. It almost seemed that the material had shrunk. Another smart practice is to slightly lift the insole of the shoes to allow the cushioning to air out and decompress after each run. This will help to extend the life of the cushioning. Just be aware that in some models the insole is glued to the shoe. In this case don't try to pull the insole as you may damage the shoe. You can always vent the shoes by pulling the tongue up.

It is also a good habit to check your running shoes before putting them on for a run. This should only take a few seconds. You want to find out if something is wrong before you are in the middle of the run several miles away from home. Check that the shoe lacing is properly tied. Look at the inside for anything unusual. Check the wear on the sole, both inside and out. These are just some clues to ensure that you have a safe and joyful run. When I go to a race or do a run far away from home, I usually bring an extra pair of running shoes. It is one more thing to bring, but if something happens that I need the extra pair I will be prepared.

As our running career goes on we will accumulate more shoes than we need. When wondering what to do with retired shoes you may donate them to an organization that can give them to people in need. The idea is to recycle the retired shoes to people that can use them for walking or leisure, and since the exterior part of the shoes still looks good they can get more use out of them.

**Essential Clothes**

A few running clothes you will need are shorts, tee-shirts, and socks. Today, the majority of these clothes are made with moisture control fabrics. These newer fiber materials are lighter, allow more air circulation and are designed to move perspiration and moisture away from the body. Most running shorts have a Coolmax® liner and nylon Supplex® on the outside. This combination provides good comfort keeping the skin cool and dry during the run. In the past shorts kept moisture in the liner making your body feel sticky and sweatier. There are many styles of running shorts and brands for both women and men. The best thing is to go to a running store and try out various styles and designs until you find the ones you like. Before buying check the label to make sure that the shorts contain one of the latest moisture control fabrics. Prices can range greatly depending on the features, style, and brand. Usually you can find good deals at Running Expos. I recommend that you get at least two running shorts so that you can alternate them. I keep several running shorts for my training and have a couple more I use only for races.

Most race tee-shirts are made of 100% pre-shrunk cotton. Cotton tee-shirts tend to shrink a little when washed in hot water and put in the dryer. If you can, wash them in cold or warm water and dry them at low temperature. The biggest problem with cotton tee-shirts is that they retain moisture. As they get wet with sweat they feel heavy and stick to the skin. This is okay during training runs but it can make a big difference in races or longer runs when you need air circulation through your shirt to cool you down. The sweaty cotton tee-shirt sticks to your body preventing good air flow. On the other hand there are many singlets made with the newer fabrics that keep moisture away. For races or longer runs, I recommend singlets made with one of these special materials. These specially designed tank-tops allow more air to flow through them and don't stick to your skin. Like shorts, singlets should be washed in cold water and allowed to drip dry to avoid damaging the delicate fibers. I keep a stock of singlets for my races. There are many brands of singlets available. Usually the same makers of running shorts make singlets. Check with your local running store for the latest types of fabrics and designs. Several years ago I was wearing cotton tee-shirts in my races. The first time that I wore a Coolmax® singlet, I noticed a huge improvement. The increased air circulation through my shirt created a nice cooling effect, which made me feel like I was carrying ten fewer pounds.

Most sport socks are made with a blend of cotton and polyester. These are fine for training or if you want to minimize the investment in running apparel. For this I would recommend that you get thin crew style socks so that they fit comfortably in your running shoes. The problem with some cotton socks is that they are bulky and hold moisture longer as with most cotton-based clothing. For races or the more sophisticated runner, a new line of running socks is now available. Their moisture control fabric contents make these socks great to keep feet dry and prevent blisters. There are several styles and brands of running socks. Some are thick, others thin, and some have a reinforced toe area. I use the thin moisture control fabric socks for races since they keep my feet dry and comfortable during the race. For training I prefer the thicker cotton socks to give me extra cushioning.

## Sports Bra (for women only)

The sports bra became a reality in the late 70s with the invention of the jogging bra. Today, there are many brands and types of sports bras on the market. Some are better for running than others. Sports bras are built for low, medium, and high impact sports. Since running is a high impact activity, you should keep this in mind when looking for the right bra. As with other running clothing sports bras are now available with the latest moisture control fabrics, which help keep you dry longer during exercise. For advice you may want to ask other female runners about which bras they prefer. Visit a running specialty store or a sporting goods store for the best selection of sports bras. Ask the female sales staff for any specific questions. Take time to try them out in the dressing room by jogging in place. Try several models until you find the best one for you. Look for comfortable support that is not overly tight. The ideal bra is one that you are not much aware of when you run.

All your running clothes should last longer if you wash them at low temperatures and drip dry them. If you must use the dryer then use a low temperature to avoid damaging the special fibers. For the most part your running clothes won't shrink unless they are blended with cotton. I drip dry all my running outfits except for cotton tee-shirts, which I get one size bigger since I expect them to shrink a little. To be safe always read the label on running clothes for adequate care.

## Nasal Strips

This is a little plastic band that looks like a bandage strip. This device has an adhesive line and when placed correctly over your nose it will pull your nose gently opening the nasal passages. The end effect is that you can breathe better and perhaps improve your performance on the road since you are getting more oxygen with less effort. The truth is that I was skeptical about this for a long time, but I hadn't tried it either. One day I decided to see for myself. Right away I noticed an improvement in the amount of air I was breathing in. I felt like I could breathe through my nose without effort. The run felt great and I had no need to breathe through my mouth. I believe that the nasal strips do increase the flow of air for most people, but the overall improvement varies from person to person. In my case it made a big difference because of my year round allergies and my narrow nasal passages. It is best to check it out for yourself and see if you notice any difference.

## Sports Watches

Although this is not an essential running item I always wear a sports watch in both my training and race runs. I use it to time my training runs for later reference. In races I use the memory lap function to time my splits and race time. I later store this information in my running log which helps me keep track of my running performance. If timing yourself is not important then perhaps you won't need a sports watch. On the other hand, I feel a watch can be used as a monitoring tool of your progress as a runner. As a beginner it is satisfying to see your times improve.

During the last six years I have used sports watches with lap memory. The first one was rather basic with one lap memory and a stop watch function. My second watch was more sophisticated with 30-lap memory. This allowed me to measure up to 30 splits. A split can be any distance that you choose to measure. Most runners measure mile splits. So, one split equals one mile. Having memory to store 30 laps is sufficient for most conventional long distances including the marathon. This means that you could measure your time in each of the 26 miles. There are sports watches with 100-lap memory and data link features to transfer the data to your computer. I haven't found the need to get one yet. You can find a good selection of sports watches in most sports stores and large retailers. As with everything else there are several brands and models available. Make sure that the watch you are selecting has at least the number of memory laps that you will need. If possible avoid the 8-lap memory watches since in a few months you will probably wish that you had bought one with more lap memory. Because timing myself is important whenever I go to a race I wear a sports watch. At home I keep two sports watches so if the battery should run out on one, I can use the other one.

**Other Accessories**

If you plan to run early in the morning or late in the evening you should consider getting reflective gear. Some of the most useful items are the reflective vests and reflective strips to wrap around your ankles. Some runners carry a flashlight when running in the dark. Be smart when running with little visibility. For cold weather running there is a whole line of specially designed jackets, long pants, gloves and hats. These are made with the latest fabrics to provide comfort while keeping you warm. Since in Northeast Florida the winter is mild I personally don't worry much about these things. Whenever it is cold I just put on a long sleeve tee-shirt and sweatpants. For specific information on cold weather items ask the staff at the local running store.

A heart rate monitor consists of a transmission belt, which is strapped around your chest and a receiver wristwatch. This device provides you with instant feedback on how fast your heart is beating during the workout. They are lightweight and waterproof. You can find these at most sporting goods stores. There are several models available ranging from a very simple heart beat monitor to top of the line versions with time, date, stop watch, lap, and other features. Personally, I don't wear this device because I would be too concerned with the heart rate feedback. I feel that my running would be psychologically limited by the feedback. I am not against using this device. I believe it is very useful for some runners, and it can be a great tool to monitor performance. A heart rate monitor can help you customize your training using the heart rate feedback as a control guide. For example, running a mile at 9-minute pace is not the same for two people. One runner may need to work harder to keep the same per mile pace. Using the heart rate monitor both runners can run the mile measuring their effort by targeting a specific heart rate instead of a minutes-per-mile indicator. This is a very interesting concept, but it requires a lot of discipline and consistency. This wireless device uses batteries that go in the transmission belt. The batteries are built to last several years but once used up they cannot be replaced. The entire transmission belt must be changed. This can get a little expensive.

In recent years with the technological revolution there has been a growing number of gadgets available on the market that claim to improve and assist the running activity. Beware of products that claim to easily enhance your running abilities. Some of the beauty of running is its simplicity. In my opinion it should be kept that way with only the essential items to make your running experience pleasant, lifelong and safe.

**Best Places to Buy**

Whether you are looking for shoes or running clothes, I believe the best place to start is a running store. These stores offer greater variety of running products and the sales people, usually runners themselves, can offer first hand experience of the products and are more knowledgeable of runners' needs. If you know what you are looking for sometimes you can save a few dollars at chain sporting stores but you won't get the same level of personalized service as in the specialty stores. Additionally, at chain stores the sales staff may not be as familiar with the running gear and specific needs of runners. Overall the specialty stores offer more selection and better service. For some people these subtleties are well worth the extra dollars. Basically at running stores you will have fewer risks of going home with the wrong stuff.

In Jacksonville, Florida the best running store is 1st Place Sports. They have two stores, one located near the corner of Baymeadows Road and San Jose Boulevard and the other in the Sawgrass Village shopping center in Ponte Vedra. The sales staff is very knowledgeable and helpful. In St. Augustine, FunRun Sports has a complete line of running gear and shoes. There are several more sports stores in Northeast Florida. The key is to go when they are having a special sale. Sometimes you find running items at considerably lower prices. In addition, Running Expos are another place to get good deals on running gear. Here you have several retailers offering running products at very reasonable prices. Running Expos are usually held during major races and marathons. In Jacksonville, the River Run Expo is done every year in March during the week of the 15K race. If none of the above are available in your area or if you want more alternatives, check the yellow pages directory under the sporting goods section. Finally, one of the fastest and most reliable ways to get information is to ask other runners for recommendations to where you can get running gear in your area. I got my first pair of running shoes by asking a runner friend.

For more information on local stores in Northeast Florida see Appendix-A.

# Part Two: *Building the Foundation*

---

"Even the longest journey begins with a single step." (16th century adage)

# Chapter 4 - Training Basics

So far, I have described my running experience, listed the benefits of running, and told you why running is a very fulfilling activity for most people. In this chapter I will talk about how you can begin a running program and tailor it to your needs.

## Running Form

We are all built a little differently, so as runners we each have a unique running style. This means that running feels best when we use our own natural style. For many years experts have been studying runners in an effort to come up with the most efficient running techniques. During my years of competitive track, I spent a considerable amount of training time perfecting my running technique. Back then every movement mattered if it could save me a split second during a sprint race. For months, I worked at keeping my right arm parallel with my left arm to avoid swinging it slightly to the left and sticking my right elbow out too far. For some reason I wasn't able to change this completely. When I returned to the roads ten years later, I found myself swinging my right arm and elbow the same way as before. This led me to believe that trying to modify one's running form is not easy. Like walking, running is a mechanical function. Our body determines the best running pattern given our weight, leg length, and physical construction among other things. This information is ingrained in the brain making it difficult to alter. To try to significantly change a person's running style would in my opinion, require teaching the proper running techniques at a very early age, almost as early as the child is learning to walk. In real life this is not very practical. Today, I don't think so much about my right arm swing. Instead, I focus more on enjoying my runs and following an adequate training routine. Nevertheless, I believe some running form improvements can be made when we learn more about our own running style.

As a beginner, running may feel awkward until you get used to the dynamics of this exercise. Don't despair, running will get easier with time. Unless your goal is to be a competitive runner you don't need to be too concerned with running form. In any case use the following running principles as reference but never force yourself into a technique that doesn't feel right. Ultimately, your body will naturally determine your own running style.

The following are some general guidelines to help you maintain an efficient running form:

- Watch your stride. Let it be natural. Don't try to make longer or shorter strides than what feels right. Over-extended strides can hurt your hamstring muscles. Strengthen the leg muscles by running up hill, or doing butt kicks and high knee strides. These exercises are described in more detail later in chapter 5.

- Avoid running on the balls of your feet or toes. Make sure that you have good running shoes and don't be afraid to step forward. Be aware of your foot flare. This has to do with the feet stepping not straight but with a little side angle, or turned out. This condition will steal a few yards from you every mile.

- Avoid hitting the ground too hard with your feet. Try to step lightly and quickly. If you are making a lot of noise then you are pounding the ground. Try to make little noise when you hit the ground, but step firmly.

- Focus on moving forward when you run. Swing arms straight back and forth not sideways. Keep arms parallel and close to your body with elbows bent in a 90-degree angle. Arm swing is very important to maintain proper balance and use the momentum of the running motion to take you forward.

- Don't clench your fists. A tight fist posture will keep you more tense and will make you lose momentum. The hands should be kept either extended or cupped. Pretend that you are holding a penny between the thumb and index fingers. Try this with a real penny to force yourself to maintain this hand position.

- Watch your posture. Your body should be straight up and slightly forward. In other words keep an upright position but lean forward slightly, about 5% to compensate for air resistance. Avoid leaning forward too much since this will shorten your stride and require more energy. Keep shoulders and neck relaxed. Keep your head straight and look ahead 30-50 feet in front, not down to your feet.

An easy way to check your form is to run on a treadmill in front of a mirror or have someone film you running a short distance on a track, at a park or on a road. This allows you to easily see yourself in action and make adjustments to your running form. Another option is to go to a sports physician for a complete running analysis. In Northeast Florida there are several sports physicians and chiropractors that offer a complete fitness evaluation including video taping of your running form. A video analysis can determine your foot flare and help you find potential areas for improvement in your running style.

Finally, keep in mind that there is no one absolute correct running style for everyone. The best approach is to experiment with these running principles. Start by observing your running form on your next run. See if there is anything that can be improved but above all let your body be the guide and keep running naturally and relaxed.

**Don't Forget to Breathe**

Proper breathing is a very important aspect of running. Learning this technique can greatly benefit your running. As a beginner, it may seem difficult to accomplish good breathing in your runs when all you can do is gasp for air and your main concern is to be able to finish the run. Well, don't worry. As you build your running base you will be able to concentrate on things such as running form and more efficient breathing techniques.

During a run as in any upright position we tend to breathe from the chest. This is different than when we sleep or lie down, in which case we breathe deeper using the stomach muscles. Breathing from the stomach allows more air into our lungs, than when we breathe from the chest. In other words, the air capacity is greatly increased by using the abdominal muscles to help expand our lungs. This in turn can help us run smoother by breathing more efficiently. By using this technique you will notice that you can run longer and feel less tired during the run. This is because more oxygen is available in your lungs and muscles.

The technique is simple. When running, inhale air through your nose and exhale through your mouth. As you inhale push the muscles of your stomach out. This will expand your diaphragm muscles allowing more oxygen to flow in your lungs. The diaphragm is a layer between the abdomen and the lungs. As you exhale bring the stomach in tightening the abdominal muscles. This will clear more air out of your lungs leaving them ready for the next inhalation. Try to relax when you use this technique to gain a breathing rhythm.

At first, this may feel odd but as you practice and get used to it, you will notice the great benefits of this technique. Eventually you will learn to breathe naturally with your stomach during your runs. An easy way to learn this technique is to lie down on your back and relax for a few minutes. Then observe your breathing, and notice how you are using the stomach muscles to breathe just like I described above. Now that you have experienced this technique, go and practice it in your next run.

When I first tried this technique it wasn't easy. It took a big effort on my part to learn it. It was confusing and felt awkward. I would start my runs practicing this breathing but after a few miles I would get distracted and subconsciously switch to chest breathing. I had to force myself back and get into the breathing rhythm again. It took me several months to make it a habit. Now I don't have to try so hard. It is part of my running technique. A few months after adopting this breathing technique I tested the difference in a 5K race. I cut my PR time by 2 minutes.

## Training Plans

In my running experience I have come across multiple training programs. In fact there are entire books written about this topic, so I intend not to repeat the same detail of training programs that you can find elsewhere. If you are interested in more detail visit your local library, bookstore or check the Internet for information on training plans. For a list of more resources see Appendix-A.

I believe that a good training plan is one that meets your fitness needs and keeps you motivated so that you continue running. A training program has to be simple so that it is easy to follow and flexible so that you have the freedom to experiment with different running routines. Using this approach you will eventually find what works best for you.

The truth is that creating your own training plan is easier than it seems. All you need is to decide up front how many days and miles you want to run per week. Then take the total number of miles per week and divide it by the number of days you expect to run each week. If you are a beginner, start with 3 days. Eventually build up to 4 days of running per week. I personally don't recommend anyone running more than 5 days per week unless you are a serious runner with specific competitive goals and have lots of time. Experience has shown me that we are not running machines. Running is good for us, but we need rest days in between.

An important factor when planning your training is to ask yourself what kind of running you want to do. Are you training just for fun or do you have racing in mind? If you are planning to race then think of the distances you will be racing. If you are a beginner, start with shorter distances like the 5K. With a defined objective it will be very easy to tailor your training plan to meet your goals. I like the under 15K races, so my training is geared for these distances. Once you start training avoid increasing your weekly mileage by more than 10% per week. After each increase stay a few weeks at the new level before the next increase. This will allow your body to adjust to the higher mileage smoothly. There are several ways to divide your weekly mileage into the number of miles per day. A popular way is to allocate one of your days as a long run when you will do more miles than the other days. Let's take for example two schedules: a 3-day running plan, and a 4-day plan. Let's say that our mileage goal will be between 12-16 miles per week.

The two sample beginner schedules are illustrated in the following table.

| 3-day Schedule | | 4-day Schedule | |
|---|---|---|---|
| **Action** | **Distance** | **Action** | **Distance** |
| 1$^{st}$ running day | 3.5 miles | 1$^{st}$ running day | 3.5 miles |
| (rest day) | | (rest day) | |
| 2$^{nd}$ running day | 4 miles | 2$^{nd}$ running day | 4 miles |
| (rest day) | | 3$^{rd}$ running day | 3.5 miles |
| 3$^{rd}$ running day | 5 miles (long run) | (rest day) | |
| (rest day) | | 4$^{th}$ running day | 5 miles (long run) |
| (rest day) | | (rest day) | |
| | | | |
| **\* Total running week** | 12.5 miles | **\* Total running week** | 16 miles |

These are just a couple of examples to show you that making your own training plan is not difficult. The rule of thumb is to alternate easy-medium days with medium-hard days and with rest days in between.

If you plan to race then your training schedule should include conditioning for the race distances you expect to do. In my experience the more you simulate the conditions of the race in your training the better your performance will be. For example, if the race is a beach run you should do a few training runs on the beach to get used to running on sand. If the race is hilly do some hill training on a treadmill with inclination or find a hill or bridge to run up/down. If your goal is to run a longer distance like the half marathon and plan to use a sports energy bar during the race, do the same in your long runs to see how your body reacts to the food. Basically you want your body to be prepared for the conditions on race day. Obviously we can't anticipate every circumstance, but we can minimize unpleasant surprises by simulating the race terrain and conditions in our preparation.

So far, I have purposely not mentioned marathon training. First, as a beginner you should wait at least one year of running before thinking of the marathon distance. If you are interested in the marathon start with the shorter distances and build up to the half marathon and eventually the full marathon. I believe the marathon is a great experience for most runners but it takes months of physical and mental preparation to reach the running level required for this distance. The marathon is such a big topic that there are entire books written about it. My advice is to read a couple of those books before you start training for this type of running challenge.

## A Plan that Works for Me

In my middle 30s, I see myself as a serious average runner, one trying to stay in the front of the pack. I am not training to be an elite runner, nor am I training to lose a few pounds. I train mainly because I enjoy running and want to stay in good shape without overdoing it. Some runners train for marathons or ultra long distance races. I am not one of them. If you are an average runner of any level you could benefit from this plan. As with any training plan feel free to modify it to meet your specific running goals.

Since I started road running I have tried several training programs. In the beginning I started running a few miles per week to condition my body to long distance running. At the time, I was practicing martial arts twice per week so I thought I was in good shape, but to my surprise I found out that the muscles required for running were very different than the ones needed for the speed and endurance of martial arts. During the first few weeks of running, my legs, thighs and calves were very sore. One day feeling strong and confident, I made plans with a runner friend to join him on his noon run. I was able to keep his pace for the first half mile. For the remainder of the 4-mile run, I was barely running and had to walk at some point. I apologized to my friend and realized how out of running shape I was. As I began to accumulate more mileage the soreness disappeared. During the first 2 years I ran an average of 6 to 10 miles per week. In my third year I increased the weekly mileage to 15 miles and ran several road races to make my training more fun. I used the races for speed training and practiced "fartlek" once per week. Fartlek is a Swedish word, which means 'speed play'. It consists of speeding up for short distances during your regular runs. It is a fun form of speed training. For example, while running pick a reference point such as a telephone pole and accelerate your speed until you reach it. Then slow down for a while and start again when you feel like it. Fartlek is a form of interval training but not quite as exact. Interval training is done over a measured distance, which allows you to be more in control of your pace by knowing exactly the distance you are running.

For the next three years I experimented with my weekly training plan going from 3 to 6 days of running. My mileage varied from 15 up to 30 miles when I was training for my first marathon. After the marathon and the three grueling months of training, I felt physically exhausted and a little burned out. I was more prone to injuries and my speed had taken a big hit. At this point I cut back on training until I felt strong again. It took me six months to rebuild myself back to the level I was before the marathon. I did it partly by running slowly and allowing more rest days. Now, after several years of road running and having completed many races, my experience tells me that my optimum training plan is a moderate one. High mileage training takes a big toll on my body and I become more prone to overuse injuries making running less enjoyable. I found that as I increased to over 25 miles per week, my knees started to hurt considerably. With this in mind I decided to settle for 4 days of running per week averaging 15-20 miles total. This is equivalent to 60-80 miles per month, which is still a significant number of miles. I like this schedule because it gives me plenty of room for rest with a day off every other day. On my day off I cross train or just take it easy. This program blends well with my fitness aspirations including my racing goals. I have chosen to train for the shorter end of long distance races, mainly the 5K event.

Whenever I decide to run a longer race I gradually modify my training schedule, adding an extra day or increasing my long run to match the longer race distance. When I decided to run the 1999 Disney World half marathon, I increased each run by 1 mile and included a series of longer runs as part of my 9-week conditioning. Overall, I went from a 15-mile per week schedule to doing 20-22 miles on the average. My long runs were gradually increased from 5 miles to 6, 7, and 9 miles including a couple of 10 milers. Doing these long runs showed me how much more effort is required for the longer distances. Being used to running 4 and 5 milers every week you don't really appreciate the difference. At first my knees hurt after 7 miles in the long runs, but I knew that it would just take time for them to get used to it. Since preparing for the half marathon and longer distances requires a lot of additional miles we tend to focus more on mileage and forget about speed. In fact, I believe we get slower. To compensate for this problem I signed up for two races during my preparation, a 10K and a 5K. I ran both at a good pace for my current condition. I averaged 7:10 per mile on the 10K and 6:55 per mile on the 5K. My goal was to run the half marathon in under one hour 45 minutes. The important part is to train according to your level and goals. After a hard week of training or a race I usually take two days of rest. This allows my muscles to rebuild themselves for the next run. Whenever I do this I find myself running stronger and lighter. My leg muscles feel rested and renewed.

I believe that each runner has a different threshold for the mileage that his body will take without getting injured. This threshold is related to body build, weight, age, health, running form and endurance. Experience has shown me that when planning a 4-day training schedule it is better to set specific days of the week as running days as opposed to running every other day. This way we have a consistent schedule every week. Otherwise some weeks you may end up running only 3 days if you go alternate days. Plus with designated running days it is easier to blend training with the rest of your life activities. With time and practice you will find your optimum mileage per week that will allow you to achieve your fitness and running goals while avoiding overuse injuries.

Following are the details of a series of stretching and endurance exercises for the legs, neck and lower back muscles. I usually do some of these before and after my runs. They only take me 5-10 minutes to complete.

• Groin stretch: Sit on the floor with the soles of your feet together. Bend over slowly resting your elbows against your thighs or knees and push your knees toward the floor. Keep your back straight as you bend. You should feel pressure in the groin area. Hold for 10 seconds then relax. Repeat three times.

- Toe touch: Sit on the floor with your right leg straight without locking your knee and bend your left leg so that your left foot touches your right thigh. Bend over slowly at the waist with your arms straight trying to touch your right toes. Hold this position for a few seconds then return your upper body to an upright position and repeat the exercise three times. Then switch legs to work the left leg and repeat the same routine. Don't forget to breathe and relax during this exercise. When you bend forward at the waist you should feel a pull in the back of your stretched leg and lower back area above the buttocks. This exercise is good for hamstrings, calves, hips, and lower back muscles.

- Calves and thighs stretch: Standing with your feet flat on the ground, place your right foot stepping in front about two or three feet from the left foot. Bend your right leg and knee keeping your right foot flat on the ground. Keep the left leg straight back with the left foot flat. You should feel a pull on your calf muscle of the left leg. Keep your upper body straight with arms on each hip for balance. The bent knee should form a right angle with the foot in front. Never allow the bent knee to go forward further than the toes in front since this puts too much pressure on the knee. Hold this position for 20 seconds then switch legs. This exercise will work the calves and thigh muscles.

- Lateral upper body stretch: Standing straight extend your right arm over your head touching your left ear. Keep your left arm hanging to your left side. Lean to your left side until your left arm extends down close to your left knee. Hold this position for 5 seconds. Return to upright position. Repeat three times. Switch arms and work the other side. This exercise will work your neck, shoulders, hips, and upper back muscles.

A couple of times per week I do a series of abdominal and upper body exercises in addition to my stretching routine. The best time to do these exercises is after the run since your muscles will be warmed up.

- Lower back endurance: Lie flat on your stomach. Keep both legs extended with feet touching the floor. Bring both arms behind your head barely touching it and keeping your elbows off the floor. Without putting pressure on your neck lift your head and chest until you feel the pressure on your lower back and hips. Hold for 3 seconds and return to the flat position without letting your arms go. Your chin should barely rest on the floor. Do two sets of 5 repetitions with one minute of rest in between sets. With time increase to three sets of 5, or two sets of 8. This exercise will build the muscles in your lower back, which are very important for runners since the lower back acts as the shock absorber of the body. The impact of every stride we make is absorbed by the lower back muscles first. Weak muscles are usually the cause of lower back pain.

- Lower back stretch: Stand with legs apart about two shoulder lengths. Keep feet pointing forward. Keeping your back and head straight bend down and with your arms extended to each side try to touch each foot with hands. You should feel a pull on your calves, buttocks and lower back muscles. Hold this position 5 seconds, then return to upright position keeping your legs apart. Repeat three times. This exercise should be done after your muscles are warmed up to avoid excessive pressure on your lower back. A slight variation of this exercise is to touch your foot with the opposite hand alternating each side.

- Crunches: There are several variations of crunches or sit-ups. The ones I like minimize the pressure on the lower back muscles while working out the abdominal area. Lie on the floor on your back. Bend both knees keeping feet flat on the floor. Cross your hands on your chest or put them on the side of your head. Raise your upper body and shoulders until they are off the floor. Hold this position for 1 second, then lower yourself back to the original position. Repeat this 10 to 20 times. Do two or three sets with 2 minutes of rest in between. An alternative way to increase the effectiveness of this exercise is to do the crunches with your legs raised bent at the knees in a 90-degree angle with the thighs. This exercise is important because it builds the abdominal muscles protecting your back by balancing the muscles from the stomach with the lower back.

- Push-ups: Lie on your stomach with your legs and feet together. Your palms should be flat on the floor parallel to your shoulders with your fingers pointing forward. Keep hands a shoulder's length apart. The weight of your body should be supported on your hands and toes. Keep your body straight with your head facing the floor. Slowly raise your body until your arms are straight without locking the elbows, then lower yourself down without touching the floor and repeat again. Do two or three sets of 10. Remember to breathe during each repetition. This exercise is one of the easiest and most effective ways to strengthen the upper body muscles. This will develop the chest, upper back, shoulders, and arms.

- Shoulder stretch: Standing straight with your arms hanging to the sides loose, shrug your shoulders up tightening the neck and shoulder muscles. Hold for 3 seconds then relax. Repeat three times.

- Neck stretch: Standing straight with arms hanging to your sides slowly let your head lean to your left shoulder. Hold this position for 2 seconds. Bring your head slowly up and lean your head to the right shoulder. Hold for 2 seconds and return your head slowly back to upright position. Repeat this routine three times. Once you have completed the side neck stretch you can do a similar routine but this time let your head lean forward trying to touch your chest with your chin. Hold this position for 2 seconds then bring head slowly up. Repeat three times. The last neck exercise is to very slowly rotate your head around your shoulders in a long circular motion. To avoid feeling dizzy rotate slowly to the left completing one full circle. Then rotate to the right completing a full circle. Do a couple of rotations to each side only. These stretches will work various neck and shoulder muscles.

- Total stretch: Lie on your back with arms and legs completely extended. Stretch your arms and legs out by pointing your fingers and toes away from you. Hold this position for a few seconds, then relax. Repeat three times.

What I have shown you so far are just a few stretching exercises available. These are the ones that I find complement my running best without taking a lot of extra time. There are many more exercises designed to work different muscles in your body. You can find more related references in sports books, running magazines, and the Internet. Additionally, most fitness centers and sports clinics give free handouts with the basic stretching exercises. Experience and practice will help you find the exercises that work best for you.

One thing I always do after every run is to walk for a few minutes to cool down. I never stop and sit down right away no matter how tired I am. This is a good habit to learn. Walking helps your whole body cool down more smoothly. After the cool down period I usually stretch my legs for a few minutes with some of the exercises mentioned above. In addition to my overall endurance training I do upper body weight lifting for 15-20 minutes once per week. I work on strengthening exercises for my back, chest, and arm muscles. I use light to medium weights. As runner my intention is not to build a lot of upper body muscles with heavy weights. Some days I combine my weight routine with repetitions in a workout machine that you use by pulling your own weight in a riding motion. Although the manufacturer claims that this is a total body exercise machine I believe it works out mainly the chest, upper back and thigh muscles. If you have access to a fitness center you should do the strengthening exercises on the Nautilus® machines. Ask the fitness center staff for guidance in the proper use of each machine. These people are trained and usually are glad to help.

My training plan doesn't end with the four days of running per week. Fitness is a big part of my lifestyle and of those around me. During my rest days I try to stay active. I play with my kids, go for a bike ride, roller skate, or find work around the house. At work, I walk often. I park my car purposely further away to increase my walking distance. When I can, I avoid elevators and use the stairs. Climbing stairs is in itself an excellent leg exercise. I believe walking is a very good complement to running. In this country we don't walk enough. We tend to drive everywhere, which doesn't help our overall fitness condition. In the summertime, I swim laps for 30 minutes twice per week. Other times of the year, I like to ride my bike at least once per week on one of my rest days. Recent studies have indicated that runners can improve their race speed by including a session of bike riding in their training. It makes sense since the bike exercise strengthens several leg muscles. Cross training is very good for runners since most of us tend to develop the lower body and neglect the upper body. A few years ago when I was practicing martial arts and running, I found that running was helping me do my kicks with much more power. At the same time running felt great since my upper body muscles were toned up from the martial arts practice. When I quit doing martial arts and kept on running I noticed after a while that I was getting all kinds of upper body aches. It took me a while to realize that running alone was not enough for my whole body, I needed to exercise my upper body muscles, too.

So far, I have given you a lot of information to think about. It is mostly practical and easy to apply. Always remember to allow flexibility in your training plan. If something is not working, try something different. A good running program must be adaptable. I imagine by now you must be anxious to go running and try some of these ideas. Just hold off a little more.

**Training Tips**

Over the years I have learned things through experience and sometimes the hard way. In this section I will share some advice and tips to make your running experience more enjoyable and hopefully with less bumps.

These are some simple but important principles to keep in mind when creating your training plan:

- If you are a beginner, start slow. This means set simple but reachable goals. The first three to six months of running should be easy to allow your body to adapt to the new exercises and running demands.
- Increase your weekly mileage gradually. Never make more than 10% increase per week to allow your muscles to recover from the extra mileage.
- Keep it flexible. A training program is good if it meets your needs. If you feel stuck or are not enjoying it, change it. A training program should never be fixed.

- Seek balance in your training. The idea is to accomplish your running goals while enjoying each step in the process.
- The old idea of "no pain no gain" is false. You don't have to get hurt to improve. The new philosophy is "train smarter not harder".
- Listen to your body. Use common sense. If something is not working look for alternatives. Your body knows you better.
- Don't forget to stretch regularly. This is a common mistake. I know it takes a little more time but it will make a huge difference in how you feel afterwards. Some people recommend that you stretch after running because the muscles are already warmed and you will feel less stiff after the run. I usually stretch before and after my runs. Experiment with when works best for you.
- When exercising make sure you do it on a firm surface for support. For example, avoid doing crunches on a soft surface like a bed or a sofa, otherwise you could injure your lower back or coccyx bone.
- Include a little endurance training in your program. Working with light weights will strengthen the upper body muscles, which are often forgotten by runners. Your running can definitely benefit from a stronger upper body.
- Always drink plenty of water before and after your runs. For longer than 5 miles bring water or stop to replenish fluids during the run. I am always drinking water, both at work and at home. Water is our main fuel.
- Make sure to go to the bathroom before running. You will feel a lot better during the run.
- Keep your toenails trimmed. Long toenails will dig into your skin with every stride creating small wounds. I have made this mistake and paid the price of a painful run. Don't cut them too short since this could cause other problems.
- If you feel sick or dizzy during a run, STOP immediately. Check with your doctor if necessary before running again. Remember your health is always first. Without it, running would be meaningless.
- Get regular medical checkups. Tell your doctor that you are running and how much. If you notice any health changes during your training consult your doctor as soon as possible.
- Proper training gets a boost from adequate sleep and a healthy diet. Including multi-vitamins in your diet is a smart choice.

- Keep a running log of your training runs and races. Although a running log is not required to enjoy running, it will help you plan better. Maintaining a log will allow you to look back at your running history and appreciate your accomplishments better.
- Beginners shouldn't run a marathon during their first year of running. The first year is for learning, experimenting and building a running base.
- Be courteous with runners you encounter on the road.

Most of these tips will become familiar to you after running for some time. I think that you will agree on this especially if have been running for a while. Additionally, there are a few more things I have learned through trial and error experience and just plain observation.

When going for a long training run it is a good idea to apply petroleum jelly on the areas of your body that will have a lot of friction, such as between thighs, and nipples in some cases. I found that after 5 miles of running I start feeling the friction between my thighs. Without petroleum jelly, it burns and I end up with a small laceration from the friction. Now, I always put petroleum jelly between my legs when running longer than 5 miles. This is a must for longer distances like 10K, 15K, half marathons and marathons. Nowadays, everybody is talking about the thinner ozone layer and how much more exposed to the ultraviolet rays of the sun we are. We as outdoor runners need to better protect ourselves from the sun. Apply sunscreen to protect all exposed parts of your body before going for a run, especially the face, neck, arms, and legs. The minimum SPF should be 15. Use higher SPF if you burn easily. This is especially true in hotter states like Florida. This is necessary whether sunny or cloudy. The sun's ultraviolet rays can go through clouds causing potential problems on your unprotected skin. The only exceptions are if you run at night or at dawn when the sun hasn't come out yet.

If you own more than one pair of running shoes, it is a good practice to alternate them among your weekly runs. Each pair of shoes is slightly different, so this will work different angles of the foot muscles due to the slight variation in the shoes. It will help to prevent injuries over time. I keep two good training pairs and I alternate them every other run. I keep older shoes for shorter runs and retire them to non-running activities after 300-500 miles of use. For more information on running shoes, see chapter 3.

## Training Safety

This is the most important information of this book. Safety must always come first. Keep in mind that you have only one body and it is for the most part irreplaceable. I am not trying to scare you or imply that running is dangerous. I just want you to be proactive when it comes to your safety. Avoid running on the road with traffic. Choose sidewalks, tracks, parks, trails, or other non-traffic areas. If you must run on the road with cars be extremely careful at all times. Run on the opposite side, facing traffic. This way you can see oncoming cars and move off the road if necessary. Wear visible clothing. Always run defensively. Keep in mind that between you and the car it is you who will lose more in an accident. Don't assume that cars see you. Move off the road when in doubt. Always look both ways before crossing the road. If necessary, stop and wait for cars to pass before continuing with your run. We all have heard of joggers being hit by cars. In most cases these tragic events could have been avoided if the jogger had taken more precautions.

A lot of us work full time or have activities that prevent us from running during the day. Our choices are to not run at all or to run early in the morning or late in the evening when it is dark. Wear a reflective vest or gear when running at night or early in the morning. If running on the road at night, which is very dangerous, watch for cars at all times. Remember to run on the opposite side. Don't take chances. Move off the road when cars are coming. As a driver, it is very hard to see at night when someone is on the road. It is best to assume that cars don't see you. Always give preference to the oncoming car. Again, run off the road whenever possible. Too many times I have witnessed runners taking unnecessary risks on the road. Some seem indifferent to passing cars. Remember that the road was primarily built for cars, not joggers. We are the ones that don't belong there.

Avoid personal stereos during your runs since these impair your hearing and may distract you from traffic or other hazards.

Personal safety is mainly our own responsibility. We cannot blame others if we don't act safely. The beauty of running is that we can pretty much run anywhere, anytime. This is nice and gives us a special feeling of freedom. But, we must be sensitive to the world's dangers and use common sense. Run during daylight hours as much as possible. Don't run alone in isolated unknown areas. Always tell someone or leave a note where you will be running and when you should be expected back. Carry some kind of identification and some cash or coins to make a phone call if necessary. Most running shorts come with a pocket for keys and coins. There are small wallets available that you can tie to your shoelaces. The idea is to be prepared for an emergency situation. Women should be especially cautious when running alone in isolated areas or at odd hours. A small can of pepper spray may add a little extra protection. These are sold at most sporting goods stores. When running at night see if you can get someone else to run with you. The presence of two runners is a bigger deterrent for anyone with bad intentions. If you own a dog and the dog can run, take him/her along in your night runs. Because of my work I go through periods when the only time I can run is late at night. I usually take my dog along. As soon as she sees me with my shorts on she knows is time to run. She loves it and has become my nighttime running partner. Most times I am trailing behind her.

**Training Away from Home**

Whether you are a busy person with frequent trips away from home or are planning a vacation, you can still maintain your running schedule.

The simplicity and beauty of running is that it doesn't require another player or a team of people for you to do it. It is just you and your running gear. Running gear is light and does not take a lot of room in your luggage. Usually all you really need are: running shoes, shorts, socks, and a tee-shirt. These items fit in a briefcase with no problem. You couldn't do the same with golf clubs or a tennis racquet. In fact most other sports require bulky equipment and special facilities in addition to other players. Another advantage of running is that you can do it pretty much anywhere you go, around a hotel a thousand miles away from home, or at a city park, or on the deck of a cruise ship. Every time I go away on a business trip or vacation I make sure to bring my running gear for one or two runs in my destination area. This is a way to maintain my running schedule without letting my other obligations seriously affect it. When I get to the new destination I map out a run around the area and ask the locals about safety issues I need to be aware of. This is a fun way to blend running with the trip. In addition I get to see streets and neighborhoods that I may never have visited otherwise. It is like taking a free sightseeing tour of these areas while doing my run.

In cases when because of bad weather or safety reasons I cannot go out for a run, I go to the hotel's fitness room and work out on upper body strengthening and run on the treadmill. A few months ago I was on a business trip in New Jersey, and the hotel was located next to a major highway. I looked for an area to run near the hotel but there were no sidewalks or parks, just busy roads. The day was dry and beautiful. I wanted to run outside and wouldn't just settle for the treadmill. I measured a loop of almost a mile around the perimeter of the hotel and parking lot. I ran five loops in 40 minutes and felt great having completed this unusual run. As you see, I take my running commitment everywhere I go. If you plan ahead you can always find a way to run almost anywhere you may be at the time. Next time you find yourself traveling for business or pleasure, check with the hotels before you go for fitness facilities and running areas near them. Do a little planning and you will make your trip much more exciting.

**Training Thoughts**

A lot of running books today offer training schedules that are geared more for world-class runners than for average runners. World-class runners have the time, age, physical abilities, and sponsorship money to dedicate themselves to these high mileage plans. A lot of these runners train twice per day almost seven days a week. This is not the case for most of us. Training needs to be according to your own skills and goals as runner. Some people like to run many miles per week. This is okay for many runners but I prefer to focus more on quality runs than on the quantity of miles. When doing the long runs becomes more of an obligation than an enjoyable activity perhaps it is time to review your training strategy and cut back some weekly mileage.

The truth is that very few runners can take a lot of miles without major problems. An average of 25 miles per week is more than enough mileage for most people to stay in excellent running shape. When you think that 26.2 miles is equivalent to a marathon, basically you are running one marathon every week and several each month. That's a lot of miles. Additional miles may hurt more than benefit your body and immune system. I know that what I run in a month is what some runners do in a week. These runners enjoy the high mileage training, and that is fine. I respect their choice. But for me 15-20 miles per week is what feels right. I believe each runner must do what works and feels right for them. In my opinion a high mileage program is unnecessary for most non-competitive runners. No matter what they say, running 40-50 miles per week takes a big toll on the body in the medium and long term. It is true that with the proper base training most runners can reach a high number of miles per week. But, my point is that the middle of the pack runners don't need to run 40-50 miles per week to stay in good shape. Several doctor friends have told me that at a high number of miles the risks for running injuries becomes much greater. They regularly treat high mileage runners suffering from overuse and stress injuries to the feet and knees. It doesn't seem very smart to have to take Ibuprofen or other pain-killers after every run to reduce the aches from the extra miles. When this happens, the best solution is to cut back. Running should not require any type of drugs. Let your body be the guide of your training intensity. Make your training a fun activity and not an addiction.

As I end this chapter I want to leave you with one thought. Running is only fun when we make it fun. For many runners training gets boring after months of doing the same routes and distances. There are several simple ways to make running more fun and to stay motivated. Join a local running club to meet other people with similar interests as yours. Do some of your runs with a friend. Sign up for races to have a goal to train for. Alternate your training runs in different locations such as the beach, trails, track, road, hills, etc. Even within your usual running area pick different routes to make your training more exciting. Whenever I start getting bored with my training I come up with a different place to run or sign up for a race. In Northeast Florida we don't have many hills, but we have plenty of beaches, trails, roads and bridges. No matter where you live there are a lot of places waiting to be discovered. Use your imagination.

# Chapter 5  - Competitive Training

Once you have built a base by running for at least six months, you may want to move to a more intensive level. Although many runners are happy just running leisurely, those with a strong competitive drive will want to keep improving as much as possible. The following are some very effective speed and endurance drills to help you become a stronger and faster runner. These can be included with your regular training runs. I usually do one of these in two of my weekly runs.

High knees: This exercise strengthens the hip flexors and calf muscles. You should do this after a little warm up (i.e. run/jog for 15 minutes). Start slowly lifting your knees in an exaggerated way in slow motion. Swing your arms up to keep balance as you alternate your knees and increase the momentum of the exercise. Don't worry about the strides, concentrate on lifting your knees high. Do this for 20-30 seconds then jog for 40-60 seconds and start again with another set. Do two or three sets at least once per week with one of your scheduled runs.

Hill running: A good alternative to high knee drills is running uphill. When you run uphill your stride will tend to shorten as you naturally lift your knees to adapt to the steeper surface. Keep your stride even and short. Use your arm swing to help push yourself forward and up. Avoid speeding while going uphill unless you deliberately want to make things harder for yourself. When going downhill keep your body straight. Don't lean backward. Try to relax but be careful as you gain speed. If the hill is too steep slow down by shortening your stride or simply walk down. On the other hand, if you want to gain speed lean a little forward without losing your balance. You will gain tremendous downhill speed this way. The benefit of hill training is stronger legs, especially around the calves and hamstrings muscles. Another benefit of hill training is that you will get faster. Consistent hill workouts could make a big difference in your next races. Keep your hill workouts to one per week. I believe that beginners should develop their running base before trying hill workouts. In flat areas such as Jacksonville I do my version of hill training on the downtown bridges. We have several high bridges ranging in length and levels of difficulty. This is a good alternative for me to get a hill-like workout and a change of scenery. Another option if you cannot get to a hill or bridge is to do elevation training on a treadmill. Most treadmills allow you to set different inclinations to simulate uphill surfaces. Start with an elevation that feels good, and increase it as you become acquainted with the additional effort.

Buttock Kicks: This exercise strengthens your running muscles. You should do this after warming up with a short run or alternate it with the high knees routine. For 20-30 seconds overemphasize your stride by trying to hit your buttocks with the back of your heel or get as close as possible. Jog for 40-60 seconds after each set. Do two or three sets of this at least once per week.

Intervals: Intervals are a form of speed training. This drill can help you get faster and improve your running form. It consists of running several repetitions of a measured distance at race pace or slightly faster. Pick a distance, for example, 400 meters (440 yards) and time yourself during each repetition. Start with 4-6 repetitions of the same distance. Jog or walk after each repetition to recover allowing a few minutes of rest in between repetitions. As you become more experienced increase the number of repetitions to 6-10. The best place to do interval work is on a track, such as the high school track. Here it is easy to time yourself over a measured distance several times. Intervals are different from fartlek speed drills in that the latter are done more freely and are less exact. Always make sure that your muscles are warmed up before doing any speed workout.

Tempo runs: Tempo training runs should not be attempted by beginners, since they risk injuries. I recommend this for intermediate to advanced runners who wish to improve their racing speed. Tempo runs involve running the desired race distance at a speed slightly slower than your actual racing speed. You should run at 20-40 seconds per mile slower than race speed. This exercise will train your running muscles under similar conditions to those of race day. This training principle comes from those who believe that training should be as much like competition as possible. In other words training at an almost race speed will develop your aerobic power and condition your body to a race-like effort for a race-like distance. If you are a marathoner tempo runs should not be done for the whole 26 miles distance to avoid overuse injuries. Instead run up to 14 or less miles at the faster pace. Depending on the race distance, tempo runs can be done once per week but no more than that unless you are an elite long distance runner. The key is to allow sufficient time for your muscles to recover from the increased effort. Adding these exercises to your training schedule will definitely make you a faster runner. These are simple but very effective running drills.

The following chart shows an example of my training schedule for a particular month with a 5K race at the end of the month (3.1 miles):

| | Mon | Tue | Wed | Thu | Fri | Sat | Sun | Total Miles |
|---|---|---|---|---|---|---|---|---|
| Week 1 | Rest | 4M | Rest | 3.5M | 3.5M | Rest | 5M | 16M |
| Week 2 | 3.5M | Rest | 4M | 3.5M | Rest | 6M | Rest | 17M |
| Week 3 | 3.5M | Rest | 4M | 3.5M | Rest | 6M | Rest | 17M |
| Week 4 | 3.5M | 3.5M | 4M | Rest | Rest | 5K Race | Rest | 14.1M |

## Speed Workouts

This section is for intermediate and advanced runners who would like to improve their race performance or just want to run faster. Beginning runners should abstain from speed training until they have reached an adequate level of running experience. As a general rule a beginner should complete at least six months of running before being concerned with speed. Runners with any medical condition should consult their doctor before doing any intensive speed workouts.

To run fast, train fast. There is no other secret. If you want to improve your speed you have to include speed workouts in your schedule. Experts recommend that you designate up to 10% of your total mileage for speed training. For example, if you run 25 miles per week, 2.5 miles of that should be for speed conditioning. Running long distances develops the endurance fibers of the muscles, which are needed to keep you going those long miles, but this is at the expense of the muscles' strength fibers, which you need for speed. This is why speed training is necessary to run fast in long distance races.

For several years I didn't have a scheduled speed workout in my training. My speed training consisted mainly of a few intervals and fartlek in my runs whenever I felt like it. Using this approach I reached a speed plateau about two years ago. I simply stopped making speed improvements. This became very noticeable when my race PRs kept getting older. From a 5K race pace of 6:30 per mile I struggled to keep a 6:45 to 6:50. This prompted me to change my training approach by including a speed workout in my weekly schedule. Because of the higher demands on the body from intensive training, I only do one speed session each week for the first 3 weeks of the month. The fourth week I abstain from speed work to allow the muscles to recover. This focused training has allowed me to regain my best speed level. I feel that soon I will be able to lower my personal records in several distances. I do the speed workout on the track because it allows me to easily measure the distances I'm running. My speed session consists of 6K divided as follows:

- Start with 4 laps (4x400) at 65-70% pace to warm up. This means that at this pace you should feel comfortable to maintain a conversation. Keep a steady pace through each lap.
- After the warm up take a few minutes to stretch your muscles.
- Do 4 laps (4x400) alternating speed. The first lap should be at 90-100% pace. Slow down on the next lap to 70% pace. Run the third lap at 90-100% pace. Finish the fourth lap at 70% pace. During the fast laps start slow increasing speed until desired pace is reached.

- Take a few minutes to walk. Stretch again if needed.
- Do 4 more laps (4x400). The first 2 laps (2x400) at 85-95% pace. Run the next 2 laps (2x400) at 70-75% pace.
- Take a few minutes to walk.
- Finish with 3 laps (3x400). Run the first lap (1x400) at 85%. Do the last 2 laps (2x400) at 60-70% to cool down.
- Walk for several minutes. Relax and stretch the legs and upper body.

A few important things to remember when doing intensive workouts are:

- Drink plenty of fluids (water, sport drinks) before, during and after practice.
- Pay attention to signs of dizziness or any unusual symptom that may indicate that you should stop. Listen to your body. Consult a doctor when in doubt.
- Stretching is very important for adequate muscle flexibility. The leg muscles will be pushed harder during speed sessions.
- Start slow, increasing pace as you feel comfortable. Don't go out fast from the beginning since this will only wear you out sooner.
- The pace speed is relative to each runner's condition and abilities. For example I can run at 7:50 minutes per mile and still feel comfortable. This would be around my 75% threshold. Anything faster feels less natural. At 6:40 minutes per mile I am at 90% effort while at 9:00 minutes feels more like 60%. In other words a beginner going at 10 minutes pace can be doing as much effort as a faster runner going at 8 minutes per mile. This is why it is important to learn to recognize your pace thresholds and limits. Having a feeling for your own pace will allow you to run more effectively.
- Come up with your own speed workout plan. Pick distances from 200, 400, 600, or 800 meters for the repetitions. Choose a combination of these distances to meet your needs. Put the emphasis more on quality than on quantity. I have selected the 400 and 800 meters because they are adequate for the 5K race.

Since I started training on the track, memories from my track and field years came back. I found out that there are several track and field meets for adults held in the spring and summer. Decided to test my luck, I recently bought my first pair of spike shoes since the late 70's. They do feel a lot softer. I'm currently preparing for several upcoming track and field tournaments this season. They are free and held almost every month. I can't wait to do the long jump again. In Jacksonville, the Jacksonville Track Club (JTC) hosts several open track meets at Bolles High School every year.

## Finding the Right Stride

This section is aimed for intermediate to advanced runners. All of us have a unique stride that comes out naturally when we run. Some runners have a long stride especially if they have long legs, while others have a short stride, yet most runners have an average length stride between 3-4 feet. In my days of track competition I spent countless hours training on speed and stride frequency. My longer than average stride helped me win many sprint races. But there was one runner who always beat me in races. He was shorter and had very muscular legs. His stride was very short. For every stride of mine he had to do one and a half. The difference was that his stride turnover frequency was higher than mine allowing him to beat me on the leg shuffling. In long distance running the stride length and turnover rate are very important. A lot of runners tend to overextend their stride. In some way we believe that longer strides will make us more efficient runners. Not necessarily true. A shorter stride with a faster turnover rate can yield better results in road running than an overextended stride that requires more effort and tires you out faster. I am the first one to admit that changing your stride is not easy. It is the natural way we run so we feel comfortable that way. The best approach is to at least experiment in your training with shortening the stride and increasing the turnover rate and decide if it makes a difference for you. Next time you run check your stride and see if you are overextending it. This is something we want to avoid since it will slow you down and could lead to injuries by putting too much pressure on your hamstrings.

## Running Camps

Running camps consist of living and training for a few days with a group of runners of various levels and ages at some secluded location under the supervision of trained coaches. Although these camps are not required to become a good runner, they can definitely help you improve your running form by checking what you are doing wrong or not doing. A running camp is an excellent opportunity to get professional advice and meet other runners. The camps are conducted in a relaxed and friendly atmosphere combining running workouts, lectures and social activities. Running camps have a dual goal of teaching you how to be a better runner while having a good time at the camp. Several months ago I attended Coach Roy Benson's NIKE running camp in Asheville, NC. It was a great experience to spend four days with other fellow runners and a team of first class coaches. Each day we ran through the forest trails of the Blue Ridge Mountains in teams according to our running speed and condition. Some days we did two runs per day. We had at least one lecture per day including one by a world class runner and another by a famous author runner. The program included several fun and social activities each day. One evening we went to a local restaurant, which included a country show and dancing. Another night we visited a local running store and headed for the movies after. For a farewell party the evening before our departure we ran a 5K against the local track club and had a small celebration with the locals after the race. The best aspect of the camp was the chance to meet runners from all over the country and some from other countries. I really enjoyed hearing their stories and being able to share our goals, hopes and frustrations. As runners we don't usually have the opportunity to do be so candid with other runners and the running camp provided just the right setting for this openness. Besides having a lot of fun I learned a few new tricks and techniques to improve my overall running. These camps are a definite nice option if you are looking for something different. But, I believe that you should wait at least a year of running before attending one of these events since most attendees are seasoned runners.

# Chapter 6 - When and Where to Run

One of the greatest advantages of running is that it can be done almost anywhere and anytime. All you need is your running shoes and the willingness to get out the door.

## Types of Surfaces

As a runner it is important to know the differences between the various types of surfaces you will encounter, especially from the perspectives of softness, accessibility, and safety. Some of the most common types of running surfaces in Northeast Florida are concrete, asphalt, grass, track, treadmill, sand, and dirt trail.

Concrete: A mixture of cement and rock. This is the stuff that sidewalks and major highways are made of. Because concrete is one of the hardest surfaces it delivers the greatest shock to the legs. In other words, concrete is bad for your legs, especially over a long period of time running on it. If you mostly run on concrete surfaces such as sidewalks, you will have a higher risk of getting overuse injuries. Sidewalks are a very convenient place to run because they are easy available, usually flat and keep us away from traffic. The problem is that most sidewalks are made of concrete. One year I did the majority of my runs on the concrete sidewalk trails around my subdivision. After a few months I started having problems with my legs and lower back because of the constant pounding on the concrete. When I eventually switched to other surfaces the aching went almost completely away. My recommendation is to avoid sidewalks or concrete surfaces if possible. If you have no alternative, try to combine with other softer surfaces, and make sure that you have cushioned shoes. Concrete is by far the worst surface for runners. A recent study rated concrete many times harder than asphalt.

Asphalt: A mixture of tar, gravel, and rock. This is the stuff that most suburban streets and rural roads are made of. It is one of the most popular surfaces among runners because the majority of road races are conducted on this surface, and most of us run on these roads. Asphalt is softer than concrete and easier on your legs. Asphalt roads are convenient and can be found around our homes and neighborhoods. I do many of my runs on asphalt roads since I don't have to travel far to find them. I just walk to the end of my driveway. When possible choose this surface over concrete but make sure that it is safe. Avoid running on roads with a lot of traffic. Always run defensively and wear reflective gear. Alternate sides of the road to compensate for the uneven gait caused by the crown of the road, but make sure that you run in the opposite direction of oncoming traffic. This will allow you to always see the oncoming cars. There are different types of asphalt roads varying in consistency and softness. Some have more cement and crushed rock. Others have more tar. Usually a higher tar content percentage in the mix makes the road darker and softer to runners' feet. A practical way to tell asphalt apart from a concrete road is that the former is a continuous stretch of material unlike the latter, which is built in small sections to avoid cracking. On a concrete road you can always see a line dividing the sections of concrete every few feet.

Grass: Grass can be found mainly in parks, golf courses, soccer fields, and around many homes. Grass is among the best surfaces for runners due to its gentler impact on the legs. The problem is that not many runners have access to a well-maintained grass field to run on. In addition it is very expensive to keep grass green and trimmed, and constantly running on it won't help its maintenance. Grass surfaces make running feel easier and more natural. The softness and uneven terrain of grass forces the leg muscles to work harder than on a flat surface. Over time this will help make your legs stronger. Usually, when I run on grass I get tired sooner. If you run on grass, watch out for holes that can trip you or cause an ankle sprain. If you have the opportunity to run on grass use it. Your legs and lower back will thank you.

Track: The track is a great place to do your speed workouts. Today, many high schools and colleges have tracks built of synthetic rubber materials. This is much easier on the legs than most other surfaces. It has been my experience that most schools allow local residents to use their tracks during off-hours. Check with the school administration for their restrictions and schedule. Most tracks are 400 meters (440 yards) around the infield, which is the official measurement of the Olympic track. This makes the track the perfect place to monitor your improvement over a measured distance. If you have children, another advantage of the track is that you can bring them along and let them play in the infield area while you run laps provided that this is allowed and safe. Because the track has two long curves in every lap, running continuously in the same direction puts more pressure on one side of the body. This means that the same leg and hip always receive more stress than the other side. To avoid this, make sure to switch directions often to allow equal development of the muscles in both sides of your body. Although optional, some runners may want to wear running shoes with short flat spikes for better traction on the synthetic track. I usually don't since my regular running shoes do a good job of holding me on the track. Whenever I can, I do speed training on the track because it allows me to easily time my laps. Also, the track brings me nice memories of my youth years of track and field competition. Track training can be fun and inspirational. Anyone who has seen the movie "Chariots of Fire" will feel a little more inspired running on the track. If you want a more complete training experience include track workouts in your schedule.

Treadmill: Most treadmills are found in fitness centers and at homes. The treadmill is basically an indoor exercise machine that allows you to walk or run on it. It has a rotating rubber platform that moves under your feet at preset speeds. While there are many brands and models of treadmills, they all serve a similar running/walking purpose. Some models allow you to set the terrain inclination (flat or hills), pace, speed, length of the run in minutes, miles or calories burned, and more. The treadmill can be a great indoor alternative during the cold winter or hot summer months. The rubber treadmill platform is better for your legs than other harder surfaces like asphalt or concrete. Treadmill running in front of a mirror can be helpful to check your running form and make any necessary corrections. Sometimes I find it hard to run naturally on a treadmill. I feel that I have to constantly pay attention to my pace and stride to avoid overstepping beyond the moving platform and stumbling. Treadmill running can be boring and monotonous. Some people watch TV, read, or listen to music while doing their treadmill workout. When running indoors, you tend to overheat faster, so it is a good idea to have a fan near the treadmill. I am not a big advocate of the treadmill, but I see its usefulness in many situations, like in extreme weather conditions or as hill training alternative. I rarely use the treadmill because I prefer the outdoors, and living in Florida I don't have to worry much about the winter months. My recommendation is to use it as needed, but don't make it your only running surface. Remember that running is an outdoor activity for the most part.

Sand: Running on the beach is a great feeling especially early in the morning or late in the afternoon. After the run you can jump in the ocean and relax. Running on soft sand is a great endurance exercise for the legs, but requires a big physical effort on your part. If you run on the beach do it near the edge of the water where the sand is firmer and flatter. This is a great surface to include in your training, but I wouldn't make it your primary training surface. The uneven sand will put greater stress on the leg muscles leading to more injuries over time. One time I went to run on the beach but forgot to bring my running shoes. The evening was too nice to let pass, so I decided to run barefoot. I had done this before and had sore feet for a week. I still didn't care. Running felt very natural with no shoes, no shirt, just a bathing suit and my watch, only the basics. I ran about 3.2 miles, I even passed runners wearing full gear and shoes, and my feet didn't bother me at all. After the run I jumped in the warm Atlantic Ocean and played with my kids. To my surprise the next morning I woke up feeling the effects of the shoeless run. Both calves were very sore. My feet had a couple of small blisters but no major damage was visible. Although, some runners endorse running barefoot, my experience tells me to be cautious. I don't recommend running barefoot on a regular basis, but once in a while it can be fun, especially to see that running is so basic to our human nature that it doesn't require more than you and your feet. Three days after the barefoot run my calves were still sore. I had run the day after with shoes and felt worse the next morning. I decided to take another day off to allow the calf muscles to recover. Running barefoot puts extra pressure on your legs and feet because there is no cushioning between your feet and the ground. In addition you can get blisters and cuts on your feet from shells and sand. If you are going to run regularly on sand it is best to wear shoes.

Dirt Trail: Although not an easy thing to find in urban areas, dirt trails can be found around mountains, forests, parks, and rural areas. In general, dirt is a better surface than most except for grass and the track. Dirt's natural softness can greatly reduce the shock of impact on the legs and lower back. Running on dirt can be more tiring, but it will help strengthen the calves and the ligaments around the ankles. It can be a soothing change from the asphalt of most roads. When running on a dirt trail after a rain, be careful of the slippery ground to reduce the risk of falls. The terrain of most dirt trails is uneven, so watch out for holes or roots that could cause ankle sprains or other injuries. It is a good option if you can get to a dirt trail once in a while. Living in flat urban Florida, I don't have access to hills or many parks, so this is not a regular type of training for me. I do it only a few times per year when we visit family on a small island 60 miles south of Jacksonville. There I can run on a secluded dirt trail away from people and traffic. If you run on a trail, make sure that is safe. Carry identification. Avoid running alone in isolated areas. Always tell others the route you will be taking and when you should be expected back. Use common sense.

Except for concrete, I believe all surfaces described above provide advantages enough to include them in your training plan. In theory you could measure the hardness of each surface type by dropping a rubber ball on it and observing how high the ball bounces back. The higher the bounce the harder the surface, meaning it would return a bigger shock to your body through the legs. On a softer surface the ball would bounce less, with the ground, not your body, absorbing more of the shock energy.

Depending on where you live, you may have access to several of the types of running surfaces previously described. The best approach is to alternate your runs on different surfaces in order to allow for more balanced training. Don't forget to switch the direction you run, since surfaces have different angles, which can create a muscle imbalance in your legs if you always run in the same direction and route. I do about 75% of my running on asphalt roads. The remaining 25% are split between concrete, track, and sand. I rarely run on grass since in my community the only grass fields are protected golf courses.

**Best Times to Run**

Morning (5:30am – 11:45am): An early run is an invigorating experience. It is a must if you've never tried it. When I run in the morning I feel energized by the new day unfolding in front of me. It is a great way to start the day. During my years of road running I have had the opportunity to run at most times of the day. Invariably, one of the best times is the early morning between 6am and 9:30am. This is when my body is the most rested after a good night's sleep. The temperature is several degrees lower and the air feels fresher. About 30 minutes before the run I have a slice of bread and a big glass of water, something to keep me going until breakfast. I also stretch for several minutes to loosen up my muscles. Some runners say that in the early morning it takes longer to reach full potential since we aren't completely awake. After the first mile I feel fully awake and warmed up. For some reason the morning run always feels more special than other times of the day. Perhaps it is the combination of the morning sunlight with the beauty of the surroundings, which give me a sense of total peace and awe. Although my work and personal commitments don't allow me to make all my runs in the morning I make sure to include a few morning runs in my schedule every month. Running later in the morning takes more effort. After 10:00am the temperature rises quickly, especially in Northeast Florida. I can run, but I definitely feel the difference. My body has less energy for a good run. By noon I am hungry and less prepared for the physical demands of a run.

Lunch Hour (11:45am – 2:00pm): Lunch time is definitely the worst time of the day for my runs. Whenever I run at this time I feel slower and heavier. By this time of the day I am low on energy and my body needs food, not to mention that this is usually the hottest time of the day. Sometimes, I schedule runs during this time as part of endurance training, but there is definitely a big difference in my energy level compared with the morning run. If you plan to do lunch hour runs try to eat a light snack such as a sports energy bar or similar 30-60 minutes before your run. This small boost of energy should help you have a better run. Drink plenty of water before and after to prevent dehydration problems. Wear sunscreen, especially in sunny and hot climates. This is the best way to protect your skin from the effects of prolonged sun exposure while still enjoying the outdoors.

Afternoon (2:00pm – 6:30pm): When an early morning run is not possible, the next best time for me is the late afternoon or early evening (4-7pm). At this time I seem to get a second wave of energy. Whenever I do an early evening run, I try to eat a snack one-hour before to stave off hunger during the run. As always drink lots of water before and after the exercise. I believe you should allow at least two hours after lunch for your body to digest the food and transform it into energy fuel. Unless I'm preparing for a specific race event I avoid running early in the afternoon. For me this is similar to running late in the morning, I feel slower and less motivated. Nevertheless, this may be an appropriate type of endurance training for a race to be held under similar conditions. During the winter months, you must be extra careful when running in the late afternoon as it gets dark before 5:30pm in some areas. Always wear reflective gear, run defensively, and watch out for cars.

Evening (6:30pm – 10:00pm): Evening runs are a great option for many runners and especially for people that work and cannot run in the morning. What greater way to shed the stress of the day and feel good afterward. But you have to be extra careful with traffic. Keep in mind that it is difficult for automobile drivers to see runners on the dark road. Whenever I run in the evening I wear a reflective vest and sometimes even carry a flashlight with me. A snack prior to the run is useful to add some needed energy to our bodies. If you run after dinner, make sure to wait at least two hours before running and start slowly. Running late at night may make it harder to fall asleep soon after the run. This is because exercise raises your energy level. In other words it makes you more awake.

The early morning and late afternoon times have worked well for me. Although I prefer racing in the early morning things don't always work the way we expect them. It was 4:30pm three years ago when I ran my fastest 5K race (20:18). Yet, early in the morning is when I feel strongest for a race. Use these times only as a reference. Because runners are all different, some feel best in the morning while others prefer the evening. These times may not have the same effects for all. Recent studies suggest that we perform best at the times we are used to running, be this in the morning or evening. My contention is that the body is more rested in the morning after a night of sleep. In the morning is when we have more energy to run. In the evening most runners won't be at their peak potential after a full day of activity. This may explain why most races take place early in the morning and not in the evening. Regardless, you should try running at different hours of the day until you find the ideal time for you. Compare how you feel when running in the morning versus in the evening. Look for patterns. Let your body be the guide to determine the best time. Keep in mind that peak performance requires plenty of rest and fuel in the form of adequate food, and you must be free of injuries and/or illness. Avoid running if you are sick or have the flu. A good rule of thumb is if your cold is in your chest don't run at all. The same goes if you have fever. Give your body a break to allow it to recover. If you only have a head cold then you may try to run, but stop if you feel dizzy or worse. The main point is, use common sense and remember that there will be other days to run when you get better. When in doubt ask your doctor for advice. Don't take unnecessary risks with your health. Eating prior to running is optional. I always allow at least one hour for light snacks before a run and two hours for a larger meal or before a race. This is another thing you will have to experiment with. If you keep a balanced diet and are in good health the biggest issue is then to have enough fluids in your system to prevent dehydration. Eating before or after the run is more a matter of personal choice.

## 25 Places to Run in Northeast Florida

Northeast Florida is a large, mostly flat area offering an endless number of places to run including beaches, parks, trails, roads, and bridges. Jacksonville alone is one of the largest cities in the United States with more than 840 square miles. St. Augustine, the oldest city in the nation and only 30 miles south of Jacksonville offers runners a glimpse of the past through its historic streets. Orange Park, across the St. John's river and south of Jacksonville's

Westside, has plenty of shaded roads, trails and parks. The list of local running places is long and could fill several chapters. Below I have included just a small sample of the most popular places to run in Northeast Florida. I believe every neighborhood has nice places to run. All you need to do is look around your area to find them.

Disclaimer: I have done my best to provide accurate information about these areas. Please run defensively and safely. Try to leave only footprints behind. Get a street map of Jacksonville and surrounding areas to help orient yourself. The mileage provided is approximate. Run at your own risk.

### *Jacksonville Areas*

Avondale/ Riverside area: This beautiful residential area close to downtown is located on the west side of the St. Johns River. There are many historic homes along the shaded and scenic streets. Riverside Avenue and St. Johns Avenue are two of the main streets. Run on the sidewalk. Watch for cars.

Baymeadows Area: Baymeadows Road runs east to west for several miles starting at St. John's Bluff Road and ending on San Jose Boulevard. All along this busy commercial and residential area there are plenty of sidewalks and side streets to run on. Be extra careful with traffic especially at the intersections. If you work in the Baymeadows Way district there are various shaded streets to go for a lunch time run. Drive around to familiarize yourself with the area first. Measure a loop or ask other runners for references.

Black Creek Trail: This is a 7-mile trail along the west side of US 17 from the Doctors Lake Bridge south of Orange Park to Black Creek. Most of the trail is paved, but there is a long wooden bridge section over a low portion of the trail adjacent to US 17. If you decide to drive to the trail the best way is to go to the south end of the trail which is located on US 17 about 10 miles south of I-295 right north of the Black Creek Bridge. There you will find a parking lot and a water fountain. From this point you can run north on the trail and back. There are some markers along the way to help you track your distance. Since the trail goes parallel to US 17 it is difficult to get lost, but run safely. Bring water along if you decide to go for a long run.

Bolles High School Track: This is a great place to do speed training. Bolles has a well-maintained full size synthetic track, a treat for your feet. The track is open to Jacksonville Track Club members once a week usually Wednesday evening. But, since this is a private school the best thing is to check the availability and schedule with the school or the friendly staff at 1ˢᵗ Place Sports running store.

Camp Tomahawk Park: Located in the San Jose area a few blocks from the Jewish Community Alliance club. Driving from San Jose Boulevard turn into San Clerc Road, continue all the way to San Ardo Drive. Make a left and drive until you come to the park entrance. This is a small park with a couple of softball fields and a nature walk around a shaded playground and picnic area. The loop around the park is less than a mile. The park has water and rest rooms. A nice place to let the kids play while you run around the nature trail and fields.

Downtown Bridges loop: Starting at Museum Circle in front of the MOSH (Museum of Science and History) run towards the Main Street Bridge. Go over the Main Street Bridge. As you descend the bridge go left. You will be on Independent Drive. Run pass the Jacksonville Landing. Soon after the street will change its name to Water Street. Continue straight all the way until you get to the Acosta Bridge. Go over the Acosta Bridge towards San Marco Boulevard and swerve left back to the MOSH circle. The loop is about 1.8 miles long. Repeat as many loops as desired. There is drinking water available by the Friendship Fountain between the St Johns River and the north side of the MOSH. Be aware that the Acosta Bridge has an elevation grade of 6-7 percent. This means that the road rises 6-7 feet every 100 feet. This is a high grade so be careful if you have never run uphill before. The Main Street Bridge is a little under half a mile long. The Acosta Bridge is about a mile long. Run this loop in both directions to get a more balanced muscle workout.

Doctors Lake Drive: Located in Orange Park, this is a scenic shaded paved trail with rolling hills. The trail is maintained by the

Florida Striders Track Club and the city of Orange Park. If you start at Kingsley Avenue the trail is about 4.5 miles until it ends on Park Side Avenue. There are mile markers on the pavement, which makes it easier to know where you are. Be cautious. Watch out for bicycles and other pedestrians. If you plan to run the entire loop of 9 miles bring water since the trail is long and there are no facilities along the way. This run is one of my favorites.

District 2 Regional Park: This is the old Dunes golf course that was converted into a city park. It is located in Arlington between Monument Road and McCormick Road. The main entrance is off McCormick Road about a quarter of a mile from Monument Road. The area has lots of grass fields to walk or run on and a shaded trail around the park. There is a paved road going from the main entrance to the side entrance by Monument Road. There are parking, rest rooms and water available inside the park.

FCCJ North Campus: Located on Capper Road in the Northside section of Jacksonville. The campus has a nice shaded trail with live oak and pine trees. Several cross-country races are held on this campus during the fall.

Hannah Park: Located south of the Mayport Naval Base. This oceanfront park has several trails for mountain bicycles and endurance running. This is a good option for a hill type workout. Watch for bikes and wild life. A fee may be required to get in.

Jacksonville Beaches area: Technically the beach area runs for many miles from Ponte Vedra to Mayport. The best area to run on the beach is Jacksonville Beach by the Seawalk or Pier area. From this point you can run north or south for several miles in each direction. Unless looking for an extra workout run during low tide. There are water and rest rooms at the Seawalk pavilion. The beach run is definitely a must in Northeast Florida.

Jacksonville University: Located on University Boulevard and Merrill Road. This beautiful campus has shaded rolling trails including a very challenging hill. Watch for cars and walkers. The loop around the campus is about 1.5 miles.

Mandarin Park: This is a city park located near the south end of Mandarin Road about 0.3 mile from San Jose Boulevard. The park has tennis courts, a playground, picnic areas, several nature trails, and a dock on the Julington Creek. The main trail loop is 1.7 miles long. There are water and rest rooms available by the playground area. The park is free and open daily from 5am to 10pm. This is a great place for a scenic and relaxed run.

Ortega area: This is a beautiful residential area located between route US 17, the Ortega River and the St. Johns River. This area has plenty of shaded streets to run on. Watch for cars especially if you run on US 17 and over the Roosevelt Bridge. Ortega Boulevard ends on Timuquana Road, which connects US 17 with Blanding Boulevard. There are sidewalks along most of the main roads. Watch for traffic.

River Road: Located in Orange Park, this is a scenic area with a view of the St. John's river. Start on River Road by the Orange Park Kennel club (Wells Road) and run south towards Kingsley Avenue. This is about 1.5 miles each way.

San Jose Boulevard: This tree-lined road is also known as State Road 13. It starts near the San Marco area and goes south for miles crossing many neighborhoods until it leaves Jacksonville into northern St. Johns County. There are sidewalks along a big portion of this road. Many scenic and shaded streets converge into San Jose Boulevard. Some of the side roads don't have a shoulder or sidewalk. Traffic is heavy most of the time so be very careful when running on these. The area north of Baymeadows Road is very scenic and safer for running since it has sidewalks on both sides, and is primarily residential. If you are new to the area drive around San Jose Boulevard to get an idea of where you would like to run. This area is ideal for long runs since you can literally run for miles each way. Best to bring water along. If not there are several convenience stores along the way where you can get needed fluids. Watch for traffic.

San Marco area: A charming residential and commercial area close to downtown. San Marco Boulevard, the main road, has several blocks of trendy shops and restaurants. San Marco Boulevard merges into Hendricks Avenue. On River Road you get a view of the St. Johns River before turning into a shaded residential neighborhood. There are sidewalks along most streets in the area. Watch for pedestrians, bicycles and cars. The annual 15K River Run course runs through part of this neighborhood. There is a loop of about 3 miles from San Marco Boulevard to Laverne Street to River Road to River Oaks Road to Hendricks Avenue and back to San Marco Boulevard. This is another beautiful area to include in your running schedule.

Timucuan Ecological and Historic Preserve: This park is administered by the National Park Service and located on Mount Pleasant Road about one mile southeast of Fort Caroline National Memorial. There are several shaded nature trails ranging from under a mile to 2 miles. The park is open from 8:00am until sundown. You can access the preserve following the Spanish Pond Trail from Fort Caroline or the preserve's main entrance on Mount Pleasant Road (Willie Browne Trail). This is a nice place to go for a relaxed run. Dogs are allowed but must be on a leash at all times. If you want to combine running with a little history, Fort Caroline is right next to the preserve on Fort Caroline Road. The fort and exhibits are open daily from 9am – 5pm.

University of North Florida: Located on St. John's Bluff Road about 1 mile north of Jay Turner Butler Boulevard (JTB). The campus has several nature trails. The paved loop around the main campus is under 2 miles. If running on the road make sure to watch for traffic. The university has a track available, which is usually open to any runners. The track is located near the tennis courts and the indoor swimming pool. Water and rest rooms are available.

Westside Regional Park: This city park is located on US 17 across from the Yorktown entrance to Naval Air Station Jacksonville. There are 2 miles of paved road and several dirt trails. The park is very shaded and scenic. There are picnic tables, a playground, rest rooms, water and an archery range. The park is open daily from 5am to 10pm.

***Surrounding Areas***

Guana River State Park: This natural preserve is located on A1A between Ponte Vedra Beach and Vilano Beach in St. Johns County.

The park has several trails of various lengths. The park is open from 8:00am until sundown. This is a great place if you enjoy running on trails and being close to wildlife. If you decide to venture into the park make sure to study the map of the place to avoid getting lost in the maze of trails. Run with a friend. It is safer and more fun. Bring water along.

Rails to Trails: This is an old railroad line that was converted into a recreational trail. It runs for 14.5 miles between Imeson Road near I-295 in Jacksonville and County Road 121 west of Baldwin. The trail is paved and is open to joggers, cyclists, skaters, and hikers. There is a parallel dirt trail for horseback riding. This is definitely a great place to run. Before venturing into this trail consider how far you plan to run, especially since 14.5 miles is more than half a marathon and if you have to come back that makes it more than a full marathon. An option is to run using time as your guide. For example run for 30 minutes in and then turn back. You will do a 60-minute run this way. This is the type of run that you may enjoy more doing with a friend or group of runners. Always put personal safety first and remember to bring water along.

Ravines State Park: This is a state park located in Palatka, Florida. The park has a steep ravine surrounded with beautiful vegetation. There is a 1.8-mile paved road that loops around the park. This is a great place to do hill training around the loop. There are several scenic walking trails. The park has rest rooms facilities and picnic areas. Bring the family along and spend the whole day at the park. There is a small fee to get in, but it is definitely worth it. The park is about 55 miles south of Jacksonville taking US 17 South towards Palatka. Follow the signs to the Ravines when you get to the center of town. The park is open from 8:00am until sundown.

St. Augustine areas: The historic city of St. Augustine has a special appeal for runners. Located less than an hour south of Jacksonville between US 1 and the Atlantic Ocean, the center of town area is perfect for a scenic run through streets lined with historic buildings. Most streets have sidewalks. Watch for pedestrians and heavy traffic in tourist areas. If you want to avoid the busy tourist section there are plenty of places to run across the Bridge of Lions. The St. Augustine Lighthouse area is one of them. This landmark is located off A1A about a mile from the bridge. Right near the Lighthouse is the main entrance to Anastasia State Park. This beach park is great for a relaxed run along the Atlantic Ocean. There is a small fee required for the park. Further south on A1A is St. Augustine Beach. This area has plenty of possibilities for runners. Just watch for cars and run on the sidewalks when available. Over the years St. Augustine has become one of my favorite places to visit and run. It has a magic touch that makes you want to go back for more. Besides, the historic things you see are real. This quaint city is Northeast Florida's up and coming jewel.

Van Zant Park: This rural park is located on Sandridge Road in Middleburg near Lake Asbury. There is a sand and dirt trail around the park of about 1.5 miles. There are several grass fields, picnic areas and a small lagoon. This is a nice place to go for an authentic Florida trail run, but the loose sand can be tough. The park has rest rooms and plenty of parking. If you decide to venture there make sure to bring a Clay County map since it can be hard to find if you are not familiar with the area. As always it is safer to run with a friend. When this is not possible be careful. Let other people know where you are going and when should be expected back. Bring water along.

**Finding More Places to Run**

Finding a place to run is relatively easy. Start with places near your home. Use your car to measure a few loops around your neighborhood. Establish routes with different distances for you to choose from including a long run and several shorter ones. In Northeast Florida many of the newer subdivisions have trails and sidewalks built around green areas. These along with residential roads give us a convenient place to run close to home. If you are new to the area or have just started running ask other runners for the best places to run. Check out local parks, school tracks, and beaches in your area. Another source of information is your local running store. The staff there usually has good information. Give them a try. Northeast Florida is surrounded by water, which means many bridges. In downtown Jacksonville, we have several large bridges that can be a worthy challenge for any runner. I try to do at least one different location run per month, sometimes more often depending on my time and family schedule. When choosing where to run use common sense. Last week while driving home I saw a woman running alone on Sunbeam Road in the Mandarin area. It was past 10pm and the street was not well lit. I believe that she was taking unnecessary risks to be running alone at that time of the night. Always think safety first. Don't run in unsafe areas such as heavy traffic areas, highways, isolated places, and late at night. The goal is to embrace fitness but personal safety should always come first.

## Road Hazards

When running outdoors you should always watch out for cars and other vehicles including bicycles. It is best to run defensively to ensure your safety first. Remember to wear reflective gear in the evening or early morning. Keep off the road as much as possible. Choose sidewalks over busy roads. Avoid wearing personal stereos that may block your hearing and put you more at risk for an accident. Listen to the sounds of nature instead. Keep running simple and natural. Additionally, watch for bumps in the road that may cause you to fall or sprain your foot. Running in Florida I haven't had many problems with unsupervised dogs, but I am always cautious when I see someone with a dog ahead of me. If possible I try to make enough noise to alert them of my presence or I run around them. Although I am not afraid of dogs it is difficult to know how a dog will react when running too close by. This is another reason why dogs should always be on a leash in public areas mainly for respect to other people.

The spring is a great time of the year to be outdoors especially in Northeast Florida. The weather is just right, not cold and not too hot. Around the middle of May, things continue to be great until the pesky flying bugs appear. I am talking about horse flies and yellow flies, which seem to become active in the late evening to chase dedicated runners. I really dislike these insects. The other day I went out for my daily run. It was late in the evening and kind of hot. I wanted to do an easy run because I was two days away from a race and didn't want to overheat myself. A few minutes into the run I realized I was being followed. Five huge horse flies were taking turns at raiding me. I tried to persuade them to leave by swatting at them but it didn't work. My only alternative was to speed up and outrun them. A mile later the miserable insects hadn't given up. Falling into desperation I was ready to turn back to my house when I switched the direction of my running and miraculously the nasty bugs were gone. I think running against the breeze helped me. I am not an insect expert but have found that the best way to avoid these bugs is to run in the morning or afternoon when these little creatures seem less active. Another option is to run at night. Bug repellent doesn't seem to do much to keep these insects away.

**Running in Extreme Weather**

As dedicated runners many times we'll find ourselves running in severe weather conditions. Although Northeast Florida has a relatively mild winter, we do experience several months of high heat and humidity as well as much rain. Therefore it is important to be aware of what to do in these conditions and to know when not to run outdoors. Running in hot weather is usually not a problem as long as your body is acclimated to it. Nevertheless you should take a few precautions:

- Avoid running on very hot and humid days if you are sensitive to heat, are taking prescription medicine, are ill, or have never run under similar conditions.

- Drink at least 16 oz of water or a sports drink before and after the run. It is recommended that you drink fluids during the exercise at least 8 oz every 15 minutes. I know this sounds like a bit too much especially if you are running far away. The best advice is to go easy the first few times and see how your body responds to the high heat and exercise. When it is really hot I take a 20-oz water bottle along with me to drink. Before the run I wet my head with cold water to keep me cool longer.

- Dress for the occasion. Wear as little as possible and choose light colored clothing since it absorbs less heat. There are specially designed running clothes that allow more air circulation to keep you cooler. Put on sports sunscreen to protect your skin. Some runners like to wear sports sunglasses to protect from the glare. These come in handy on sunny days running on the beach.

- Use common sense. Don't push yourself to do a hard run on really hot days. The truth is that you probably won't lower your PR and may risk getting sick instead. Give your body a break on hot days.

- Pay attention to signs of heat problems. Stop running if you feel dizzy, confused, experience nausea, sweat excessively, or observe any unusual symptoms. Consult with your doctor before resuming running again.

Luckily, in Northeast Florida we don't have to worry about extreme freezing temperatures and snow. During the winter months we get a few cold nights, but the temperature usually never goes below 22°F. This means that we can run outdoors most of the year. If you decide to run on these cold days make sure to dress appropriately. Wear long pants and a jacket or sweatshirt. Protect your hands with gloves. If the temperature is below 40°F you may want to wear a hat to cover your head and ears. For below 32°F protect your throat, mouth and nose with a scarf or ski mask. The greatest lost of body heat is through the head. If you are going to be running in cold temperatures a lot, you may want to invest in running gear designed for cold weather, but living in Northeast Florida I don't see the need for it. One condition that we do have often is rain. Running in the rain can be a fun experience if you don't mind getting wet, of course. The main precaution during a rain run is to watch out for lightning, and we do have lots of this in Northeast Florida. In fact, I believe this area is referred to as the lightning capital of the world. Lightning can kill you. My advice is don't go outdoors when there is lightning nearby. If you are caught in a lightning storm during your run, look how far away the lightning is striking. Seek cover right away. Lie down on the ground if necessary. Avoid open flat spaces and trees. When running in the rain your shoes will get wetter from stepping on puddles than from the rain itself. I tested this one time. My shoes got really wet by running through the puddles of water. Your shoes will stay dry longer if you avoid the puddles. Running with wet shoes can cause blisters on your feet.

Finally, I cannot stress enough the point that you need to drink plenty of water during your running especially in warmer climates. Get used to drinking water all the time including the days you are not running. Don't let thirst be the guide, since by then it is too late. This means that you must proactively drink water instead of waiting until you feel you need it. A dehydrated body will not perform well. You can determine the approximated amount of water you consume during a run by weighing yourself before and right after the exercise. Subtract the difference. For each pound lost your body has used about 16 oz of water. You need to replace the lost fluids.

Running in Northeast Florida you will share the roads with many runners including some local and national level celebrities that live on the First Coast. On the road there are no major distinctions among runners. We all are there because we enjoy running. Let's be courteous to each other.

Doctors Lake trail, Orange Park, Florida.

Entrance to Guana River State Park, St. Johns County, Florida.

Simply running on Northeast Florida's beautiful beaches.

Running through the woods on a rainy day.

Don't forget to stretch before and after you run.

# Part Three: *Beyond Training*

---

"You are not finished if you lose, you are finished if you quit."
(Anonymous)

# Chapter 7 - Racing

For many runners training alone is not enough to keep them motivated. Racing provides the excitement and incentive needed to make running a long lasting activity. Although I don't just train to race, racing complements my running very well. I run because I love running and race because it is fun and because I enjoy being with other runners. I know some runners don't feel the need for racing, but races are not only about competing. The atmosphere at races is so unique and special that whether you run for fun or to win there is something for you at these events. What a better way to celebrate running than being at a road race with your fellow runners. It is an unforgettable experience.

Road racing has become very popular in the nineties. Every year more race events are added to the already full calendar. This is great for runners since we have more events to choose from. No matter where you live there is likely to be one or more road races held near you. In other words, if you desire and are willing to drive a little, you can participate in a race almost every weekend of the year. There are several race schedule publications available in Northeast Florida. Chapter 8 and Appendix-A contain local race information and some useful references.

## My First Race

After four months of running my brother and I signed up for our first race, the "Bridge of Lions 5K" in St. Augustine, Florida. We had never run a road race and didn't know what to expect. I was afraid that we weren't prepared to face other runners. We arrived late in the afternoon for the evening race. Right away I was surprised to see so many people. There were runners of all ages and all sizes. Some looked in great running shape, but most looked just like normal people. We walked around trying to look experienced and blend in with the crowd. It seemed to work since nobody stared at us. Everyone was happy to be there. This was the place to be. I thought where had I been all these years to miss out on this much fun. We lined up near the front. When the race started, I found myself experiencing a whole new dimension of emotions. Here I was running with all these friendly strangers, yet I felt welcomed. Hundreds of bystanders cheered us as we fought our way up the Bridge of Lions. The first mile was not as hard as I had expected, but by the second mile I was struggling to keep a steady pace. I still managed to smile wide as I crossed the finish line feeling like a champ. I completed my first 5K race in 24 minutes. After the race we mingled with other runners while enjoying the food and drinks provided. We drank lots of fluids and ate several bananas to replenish our worn out selves. The post-race party and awards ceremony were great. Walking back to the car, a thunderstorm broke out and got us all wet. We started jogging and stepping into every puddle we found. It was our silly way to celebrate our first race experience. That evening I hadn't won a medal, but felt like a winner for having been there. From that day on I knew that road racing would be part of my running life.

**Why Race**

Runners set…GO! This is a familiar sound if you have run a road race. It signals that the excitement and competition have begun. But, why do we push our bodies to exhaustion and pain? Perhaps it is the inherent desire to win against others, or maybe to test our own limitations. I believe we all have varying degrees of a competitive streak. For some it is more intense than for others, but in general people love to compete. It is part of our human nature.

I remember many years ago in the high school track championships, my main goal was to win all my events. I had developed a strong desire for victory from years of training for this purpose. Back then I entered every track event expecting to win. To think anything less would have meant accepting defeat before trying. In reality I didn't always win but I still had to believe that

I could. At first, running road races was similar in that it revived my youthful desire for winning. I stood at the starting line thinking that I had a chance to place high in my age group and perhaps set a new personal record (PR). Every race was a new opportunity to come out feeling like a winner — to go beyond the quiet satisfaction of just completing the distance, to reach the higher feeling you get only from knowing that you gave everything you had. In other words, I would not settle for less than doing my best that day. I believe that I am not alone in this way of thinking. Many runners are competitive people. We like the thrill of running against others and our past bests. We enjoy the idea of winning and the chance to improve our times. Yet many other runners race to complete the distance or just for fun. We all have our own goals and reasons for being at the starting line. Each reason is equally important and valid. In a way all of them have something in common. Being at the race we feel powerful and different. We stand ready to take on the distance and push our limits. Crossing the finish line makes everyone of us feel like a world class athlete.

Competition can be fun and a great motivator to run. It causes us to improve, reaching higher than we ever thought possible. However, competition is only a small part of the overall running experience. There is so much more to running than winning or improving our times. Most of us race because we love to run not the other way around. Sometimes you will have a great performance while other times you may not. This is okay. It is part of the experience of racing. Even the best runners have bad days. Try to learn from each race experience, and most important, keep on running.

If you are a competitive person, it can be difficult to avoid seeing every race as a new opportunity to win against others or yourself. I must admit that it takes much effort on my part. I need races to keep running, and I need running to keep racing, so in a way this is what keeps me going week after week. Looked at from a different perspective, races represent the rewards of weeks or months of hard training. At road races I can see myself in action. I enjoy the excitement created by the race environment. Sometimes I can go without racing for a couple of months especially if I am feeling burned out. But, usually I always have a race event to look forward to in my training. When I'm feeling in good shape, I may schedule several races in a relatively short time to take advantage of my good condition. This approach allows me to reach a period of intensive competition. During this time it becomes easier to improve my PR times or at least get close. But this is not pain free. Many times during a race, when I'm pushing my body to its limits I think about slowing down and cutting back on races. This feeling doesn't last very long. A few days later I am looking forward to the next upcoming event. I guess the positive feelings of racing are stronger than the pain and sweat of the effort required.

I believe that committing to a few races throughout the year will keep you very motivated to keep running. If you are a beginner or have never raced before, try it. You will always remember your first road race. It is a wonderful experience. After I convinced my wife to start running, I told her she should sign up for a race to stay focused. She did, and ran her first 5K only three months into her running program. She liked it so much that she ran several more in the following months including the challenging 15K River Run. Today she continues to run and race regularly. It is contagious. Once you start it is difficult to ever stop doing it.

**Road Race Distances**

There are several types of road races in today's running scene. They vary mainly in distance, how often they are held and popularity. The following is a brief description of the most traditional race events you may come across.

1 mile: This is traditionally a track race. There are very few competitive 1-mile road races. For the most part the mile is associated with the fun run or kids' run in today's road races. The competitive mile race can be a very fast event so if you are a beginner don't start out too fast. It is best to start slower and pick up speed once you have reached some momentum.

5 K (3.1 mile): This is perhaps the most popular road race today. The 5K is an ideal distance for beginners and runners doing less than 15 miles per week. The shorter distance allows you to experience the joy of racing without totally wearing you down as in longer events. The body's recovery time for the 5K is usually 2-3 days. For competitive runners the 5K is a very fast race. The

relatively short distance doesn't allow much time for pace adjustments. In other words if you are running with a specific finish time goal there is not much room to recover any time lost as in longer races. For competitive runners the 5K is an all-out race. For beginners and non-competitive runners the 5K is a fun distance. The nice thing about the 5K is that almost every weekend there is one or more of these races held somewhere in Northeast Florida.

4 mile: This distance is a little more than the 5K so the effort required is very similar. This race is not as popular as the 5K but it is a good beginner race distance. In Northeast Florida there are a few of these races held throughout the year. For most runners the extra mile over the 5K gives a little more time to settle into a steady pace.

8 K and 5 mile: Although these are not exactly equivalent distances, they are very similar. The 5-mile is a few yards more than 8K. This race is a good intermediate distance for runners with several months of training who want to get into the longer distances such as the 10K and beyond. For beginners this could be a tough distance to start with. In Northeast Florida several of these events are held throughout the year. The 5-mile is usually more common than the 8K.

10 K (6.2 miles): The 10K is another popular race. It is tougher than the shorter distances. Being twice the distance of the 5K, runners have more time to recover from a slow start and still meet their time goals. Because this is a longer race more training is required to complete this distance. Beginners may have a harder time finishing this race if not well trained. Throughout the year there are a few of these race events held in Northeast Florida.

15 K (9.3 miles): This middle distance event is very popular in Northeast Florida. This is due mainly to the annual 15K River Run, which is held in Jacksonville every spring. This is a much harder distance than the races under 5 miles. Training requires longer runs and more commitment. As a beginner you should have at least 6 months of running before entering this event. Basically, it takes real stamina to run this distance. It is like running three 5Ks

together. Once you complete this distance and with a little more training you should be ready to do the half marathon.

Half Marathon (13.1 miles): The half marathon is more than twice the distance of the 10K, so it is definitely a tougher race. But, it is a great alternative if you want to run a long race like the marathon but aren't ready for the big one yet. Obviously, this type of distance requires a lot more intensive training than the shorter races. I believe you should be putting in at least 20 miles per week before attempting this distance. Otherwise, the risk of injuries is much higher. In Northeast Florida a few of these races are done throughout the year, but they are held less frequently than the shorter distances.

Marathon (26.2 miles): The classic marathon continues to be a popular race among many runners. Proof is that most of these events attract thousands of runners of all ages and levels. The only catch for marathon running is that these races are not done as often as the shorter events for obvious reasons, so if you want to run a marathon you have to travel to where they are being held. This type of distance requires months of special training and body conditioning. Running 26.2 miles is no small effort no matter how well trained you might be. This is not the type of race to be attempted without adequate preparation. The post-marathon effects will be less severe if you had a good preparation.

In addition there are a few other distances like 2-miles, 12K, and 30K among others. Several of these race events are held throughout the year in Northeast Florida, but in much less frequent numbers.

When selecting a race look at the amount of miles you are doing per week. The race distance should be in proportion to your weekly mileage. For example, if you run 15 or less miles per week and wish to do a half marathon, you may have to increase the mileage of your training to be adequately prepared for the race. If your goal is just to finish even if you have to walk then the extra mileage may not be needed, but if you have a specific time goal you will have to be prepared. Basically, the longer the race the longer your weekly runs will have to be to raise your total weekly mileage. There are specific training plans for each race distance, so this is not a big secret. One good rule of thumb is that you should do several runs of at least two thirds of the race distance in your training. So, for a half marathon you would have to include a few 9 or 10-mile runs as part of your preparation. However, the first thing is to decide what type of race distances you want to do and develop your training plan accordingly. For more information about training for specific race distances check the references in Appendix-A.

When you sign up for a race you will need to provide some personal information such as your name, address, age, gender, and a waiver of liability in case you suffer an injury during the race. This is standard information required by all road races. Although in the majority of races everyone runs together, the age and gender information is used to group runners into separate categories. The age divisions usually start with 13 years & under, and continue with groups of 5-year intervals up to 70 & over with slight variations for smaller events. Some races offer a Clydesdale division for men over 200 pounds and women over 150 pounds. Awards are given in most events to the top 3 in each age group as well as the overall winners. This system works well except when there are age groups with a much greater number of runners in it. For example in a particular race the 40-44 men group may have 85 runners while the 25-29 group has only 10 entrants. Using this award system only the first 3 runners in each age group will get a medal. So runners in the older age group will have to work much harder to be recognized. A better system is one that assigns more awards for the age categories, which traditionally draw more runners. Although I believe that the majority of runners race because they enjoy running and not because they may get a medal, it is important to recognize their effort. In general people like to be acknowledged and giving out a finisher ribbon is a low-cost and effective way to encourage repeat customers. After all unless you are a pretty fast runner, people from the middle of the pack back usually never win awards. It is often the same runners that win most race awards. A finisher ribbon would be a little recognition for those that don't have much chance of winning but loyally show up at the starting line every time.

Today many road races are USATF and RRCA certified. This means that the course distance has been officially registered and certified with these governing bodies of running. This gives more validity to the race event and any potential records that may be set on its course.

Although racing is an important aspect of the running experience, beginners should limit their race participation during the first year. This initial time should be used mainly to build a running base and become comfortable with the running routine. This is a time of great discovery for most beginners in which they will experience many of the benefits of running for the first time. As they get in shape they will feel better and more committed. Eventually they will begin to see themselves as runners. I believe that after 3-4 months of continuous training you should be able to start with shorter races like the 5K and 4M events. By the 6th month you could start moving to the intermediate distances like 5M, 10K and 15K, but only if you feel prepared for the demands of the longer races. Beginners should stay away from marathons in the first year. There will be plenty of time to attempt the 26.2-mile event. In my opinion the marathon requires a very intensive level of training, which most beginners won't attain in the first year. The risks of injuries are high and the post-marathon effects can make an inexperienced runner lose interest very quickly. The truth is that our bodies were not made for this type of running. The marathon is sort of an extreme in long distance racing and you should be physically and mentally prepared to go through this event. Even if your main goal is to run a marathon you should first do several 5K and 10K as part of your endurance training.

Several years ago when I decided to enter the New York City Marathon, I had to make drastic changes to my weekly training. First, I added an extra day of running bringing my weekly runs to 5 days. I increased my long runs to 12 and 14 miles and decided up front that my marathon goal was to finish the distance without walking. It still took over three months of hard training and mental preparation. I even ran my long runs with a belt pack to get used to real race conditions. I carried a sports gel energy bar and water to consume at the half point of my runs. I must admit that it wasn't easy, and my body eventually felt the toll of the extra miles. I remember having muscle cramps in both thighs at mile 15 on the Queensboro Bridge. The pain was so bad that I had to stop to get muscle rub cream at the first-aid station on mile 16. From that point the pain continued until the finish. Around mile 20 the pain intensified again and thoughts of dropping out increased, but my will was stronger and I kept running. Perhaps this was the "wall" for me. Once I reached Central Park at mile 23, I knew that I would cross the finish. Later that evening I realized I had bleeding and bruised toenails, blisters on both feet, a friction laceration between my thighs, and overall muscle soreness. I couldn't walk straight for several days after the race and felt lots of muscle soreness going up and down steps. Nevertheless, I felt lucky. I had heard other runners complaining of blood in their urine, and other worse effects than mine. Overall it took me many months to fully recuperate from the post-marathon effects, but it was a wonderful experience. The early bus ride to the starting line, the line up by projected finish time, the enthusiasm of runners and spectators, the feeling of greatness over the Verrazzano Bridge with 30,000 other runners, and crossing the finish line victorious after 4 tough but memorable hours. To me the marathon is in a league of its own. It requires a very different strategy and preparation. It is definitely a great experience and something to attempt at least once in your running life. For me, I know I will do another marathon in the near future.

In Jacksonville, the marathon is held every year in December. Although this is not as big as some other Northeast Florida races, it does bring several hundred runners. If you are a marathon runner this is one to include in your list. There are several running books dedicated entirely to the subject of marathon training and the marathon experience. Check your local bookstore or library. See Appendix-A for a list of running books.

Since I started running the roads I have completed close to 100 races of every traditional distance including the half marathon and marathon. I have gone through periods of running several races per month to no racing for many months. One year alone I did 25 races. But, overall I averaged about 20 races per year. I try to run at least one race per month, but sometimes I find myself entering 2 or 3 in the same month. My goal is to run between 15-20 races per year. I prefer the events under 10K. My favorite race is the 5K, but I run a few longer races up to the half marathon to vary my running. For the most part, I have stayed away from the marathon because it requires an extremely high level of training. The extra mileage needed ends up wearing my body down and makes running less enjoyable for me.

I believe the number and types of races you do is a personal choice. But, whether you decide to run 5 or 20 races per year let your body be the guide. If you are new, start slow. Whenever possible include some out-of-town races to make your running more fun. The idea is to combine running with leisure. An out-of-town event gives you a reason to visit new places. It is a change of scenery. It is an opportunity to include family or friends in your running. You can always go alone too. I have done it both ways. Many runners travel alone to races. It is usually easy to make new acquaintances at these events. This is just another opportunity to make running and racing a great experience. Give it a try. You will have fun.

## The Week Before the Race

The experience of participating in many races has taught me a few things about these fun events and how to prepare for them. The best way to prepare for a race is through adequate conditioning and training so that there are no surprises during the race. For more information on training read chapters 4 and 5. Assuming that you have adequately trained for the event there are several things you should do during the final week before the race. These tips are aimed at making your race experience more enjoyable and problem free.

- Cut down on your training. This applies to both mileage and intensity. Plan ahead to reduce the number of runs during the last week before the race. If you have not reached the optimum race conditioning by then it is too late. Trying to jam a few more miles or runs during this time will just worsen your performance on race day. At this point the best approach is to adjust your race goals and include some rest time to relax and allow your body to reach race day in good shape. Don't think everything is lost. You can still have a good race and a fun time. I have done better than expected when I least thought possible because of being under trained. The truth is that if you have been running consistently for a while and stop running for a few days you won't lose your running muscles. In fact they may rejuvenate during the down period so that when you run again they will feel strong and renewed. Avoid running on the day before the race. Some elite runners do a soft run the day before to loosen up their muscles. I prefer to relax and save all my energy for the race. With some exceptions I usually don't run on the 2 days before a race. I believe that a hard workout 48 hours before the race will just take away from your race performance. This is because the bodies of most runners need at least 40-48 hours to rebuild the muscle tissue destroyed during an intensive workout.

- If possible drive or run the race course before the race. Check if the terrain is flat or hilly. Notice the turns and any unusual features. The idea is to know what to expect on race day so that you can develop an accurate race plan. If a visit to the race location is not possible then study a map of the race. At least you can get some idea of the course by looking at a street map. Running the race course a few days before the race gives me a little advantage on race day since I already know what's ahead of every turn. Otherwise I may end up holding myself back for unknown obstacles that aren't there.

- Plan in advance your route to the race location, especially if you are not familiar with the destination. Make sure to get good directions and study a map to know how to get there on race day. You want to avoid being lost on race day. Estimate how much time it will take you to get there, and plan the time you need to leave your premises on the day of the race. If possible check out the parking at the race in advance. If parking is difficult you may need to arrive earlier or carpool with other runners. Since I started racing I have missed only one race. This happened when I underestimated the driving time and arrived 2 minutes late. It wasn't fun to get there and watch the runners leave at the sound of gun. It is a good habit to be at the race location at least 45-60 minutes before the starting time. Some popular events require that you be there two hours before the scheduled start time. This is usually stated on the race instructions. Take time to read them.

- It is always a good idea to pre-register for a race. It will save you time on race day and money since many events reward early registration by offering a lower entry fee. In addition you will be sure to get a tee-shirt of your size. Besides, you can relax more knowing that you have already signed up for the race instead of waiting until the last minute to decide. Make sure to send your completed application and payment far in advance for the mail to reach its destination on time. Whenever I decide to enter a race, I try to send my application several weeks before to ensure that there will be no problems. If the race is within a week, I go in person a couple of days before or wait until race day for onsite registration. Always follow the instructions on the race registration form. When advance registration is not possible make sure to arrive at the race location at least an hour earlier to turn in your race entry. If possible fill out the entry form in advance to save time. Keep in mind that some large races don't allow registration on race day. This should be stated on the race entry form. For payment bring the exact cash amount or a personal check. Most events don't allow credit card payment on race day. At least I haven't found one yet.

- Most events designate a race packet pick up period. This is usually done one or two days prior to the race including the day of the race in most cases. The packet contains the race number, race instructions, tee-shirt, and some other freebies. It is always a good idea to pick up your packet within this period to avoid the race day confusion.

- Check out the weather for the day and location of the race. Be prepared for unexpected weather changes right before the race. Keep in mind that the body's temperature goes up by about 20°F degrees during a run, so don't overdress. The ideal race temperature is about 55°F. In Northeast Florida we have to be more concerned with the heat and humidity than with cold weather, but if the temperature is below 45°F you may wear long sleeves or a trash bag. The trash bag is useful for cold, rain, or windy conditions. It is simple and cheap. Just take a big plastic trash bag and cut openings for the arms and head. Put it over your racing clothes and take it off during the race as needed. Another option is to wear old clothes you won't mind leaving along the course. For colder days bring extra clothes to put on after the race to prevent hypothermia.

- Because running shoes are tight it is a good idea to trim your toenails a few days before the race to avoid blisters or black toenails. Do this a couple of days before the race to allow time to correct any related problem that may come up. Don't cut the toenails too short since this can cause other problems.

- Experience tells us that is a good habit to check all your racing gear a few days before the race. Check your racing shoes, race clothing, and stopwatch if plan to use one. Familiarize yourself with the watch's features especially if you are planning to track mile splits. Otherwise you can always get your official finish time later. Avoid waiting until the day of the race to find out that your racing shoes have a problem or that your racing clothes are wet. I have made the mistake to wait until hours before the race to find out that the racing shoes I wanted to run with were coming apart. Luckily I had an extra pair. Don't let this happen to you.

- It is important to get enough sleep the days prior to the race. But don't panic if you can't sleep much due to worries about the race. This happens to many runners. You should do okay. I once ran a personal best half-marathon with only 3 hours of sleep, but I believe this was an exception. We need adequate sleep to be at peak level.

- As with any sports avoid alcohol the day before the race. Don't overeat and be sure to drink plenty of water or equivalent sports drink. Minimize the consumption of carbonated and caffeine drinks. There are several theories on the foods you should eat or avoid during the few days before the event. For years we have been told to carbo load during the week prior to a race. This consists of eating mainly pastas, cereal, and grain based food while reducing the consumption of red meat and high protein meals. Contrary to this in recent months there has been discussion that a carbo diet alone may not be as effective as originally thought. Instead a combination diet of carbos with some protein may increase performance by providing the needed fuel for the type of anaerobic exercise performed during a race. The point is to seek balance in your diet especially as you get close to race day. Definitely avoid eating foods that you are not used to on the day before the race. A while back on the night before a 1-mile race I ate a couple of plums thinking that they would give me some extra vitamin C. Instead, the next morning I was having stomach cramps and gas pain. Luckily I was okay for the race but learned my lesson to stay away from unusual foods the day before the event. The best advice is to use common sense and keep it simple. Sometimes because of the excitement of the coming event we start doing unusual things to prepare better and this is when we get in trouble. Just be yourself and enjoy the experience.

- It is best to relax the day before the race. Don't spend the day doing hard physical labor. Stay away from the sun since too much exposure will drain your energy. I usually relax listening to good music, reading, or watching an inspirational movie.

- The following is a list of items to prepare the day or night before the race. The idea here is to save time and hassles on race day. A few ahead-of-time preparations will leave you free on race day to fully concentrate on running your best.

  ✓ If driving to the race make sure that your car is ready to go and fill the gas tank the day before.
  ✓ Pack your sports bag with a change of clothes for after the race and some extra running clothes in case you need them. It is a good idea to bring an extra pair of running shoes, a towel, deodorant, a plastic bag for wet clothes, safety pins for your race number and whatever you may need before and after the run. Leave your racing outfit handy for you to quickly find it on race day.
  ✓ Pack a map or directions to the race if not familiar with its location.
  ✓ Bring a few snacks such as sports bars, bananas, and water or sports drinks.
  ✓ Don't forget to bring sunscreen. In Florida this is essential to protect your skin from the sun year round.
  ✓ Bring a jar of petroleum jelly. It will prevent blisters caused by friction, especially in long races. You will need this right before the race starts.

115

✓ Bring identification, a pen, and extra cash for emergencies.

✓ A camera may come in handy at races especially if you are bringing a friend or spouse who isn't running. They can take a memorable photo of you crossing the finish line. Every race is unique and if you think about it, there will never be another one exactly alike, so I try to take pictures whenever possible. The trick is to convince my wife to come along. If she is running then we ask someone else to take a picture of us near the finish line for posterity. It is fun and it gives us something to look back on. Someday we will show these photos to our grandchildren. Bringing a camera to races is definitely a matter of personal choice. In my case it has become a habit to have a camera around since it is easier to be prepared than not and wish I had one with me. Disposable cameras don't take up much room, are easy to use, and take good quality pictures.

## What to Do and Expect on Race Day

Race day! Congratulations. You made it! The race is only a few hours away. It takes courage and a lot of effort to come this far. Think back on the many hours of running and sweat you have completed to get here. This is a big accomplishment, and you are one of the few committed runners. Although I have participated in close to a hundred races, I always feel very happy every time, just like the first race. Racing makes me feel like a real runner. Every event is a new experience, but with the excitement comes a little anxiety. Sometimes I worry that I won't perform as expected or that something will go wrong. Having to run against other runners can be a little overwhelming for some people. But don't worry. This is normal. In fact a moderate level of anxiety is good. It becomes the catalyst to keep you more alert and ready to run. Another way to minimize the worries is to know what the race will be like and to make sure that we are prepared. In the following section I have listed a few more tips for the hours right before the race, the line up, and the minutes after you cross the finish.

• There are different opinions about pre-race meals. Some experts suggest that a light meal 2 or more hours before the event is sufficient for most people. Others say that a more

116

complete meal about 4 hours prior to the race can increase race performance by yielding more energy fuel to the body. But everyone agrees on the importance of fluid consumption before, during and after the race to minimize the risk of dehydration. I have met runners that don't eat anything before a race except drink lots of water and do fine. This is because people have different food tolerances and rates of metabolism. The best thing is to experiment with what you think will work best for you, and keep trying until you feel comfortable with something. Don't experiment with new food on race day. In my case, for morning races I eat a light breakfast (toast or a banana, and juice or water) about 2 hours before. For evening events I eat a low-fat lunch several hours before the race. If I get hungry I eat a light snack up to 2 hours before. I drink water every hour in 8-16 oz amounts. I keep doing this until a few minutes before the start. Except for fluids, I believe eating less than an hour before the start can cause indigestion or nausea during the race.

- It is normal to have to go to the bathroom very often before the race. This is usually the direct result of drinking lots of fluids and our nerves acting up. Go as much as you have to. Keep replacing lost fluids with more water or sports drinks. There will be portable bathrooms at the race site, but it is advisable to take care of your potty needs at home if you have the option. Many times there is a long line of runners at each portable bathroom.

- If you can't stop worrying about the race the best thing is to distract yourself with relaxing thoughts. Remember that the main objective of the race is to be a fun activity. I know some of us like to set high goals putting unnecessary pressure on ourselves. We must put things into perspective. A race is a race and the essence of the event is what we want to make of it. Don't fall into the trap of thinking that this is the last opportunity to achieve your goals. An effective way to reduce the anxiety is to ask yourself: what is the worst thing that can happen? Even if you have to walk the entire race you can still have fun and learn from the experience. There will always be other opportunities to race again.

- It is a good idea to apply petroleum jelly between your thighs and on any other parts of the body susceptible to friction blisters. The longer the race the more chance of getting blisters on parts rubbing against skin or clothing. For women apply petroleum jelly on the skin under the elastic band of the bra.

- Runners are a sweaty bunch, especially in Florida. You may want to bring a change of clothes and a towel for after the race. This is a matter of personal preference. I feel uncomfortable when my sweat starts to cool off, so I usually bring a towel and clothes to change.

- Many seasoned runners have their own ways or rituals for getting ready on race day. Some may drink coffee or tea before the race to get a caffeine boost to help them reach their running potential for the race. This is fine, but be aware that there are side effects to some foods. Caffeine is diuretic, and therefore it will make you lose more fluids at the time when you need to be fully hydrated. Just be aware of what you eat or do right before and how this may be hindering your performance or health. Some over-the-counter drugs can get you disqualified from the race if you were tested positive.

- I have said this before, and I'll say it again. Drink water before, during and after a race. It is very important to stay hydrated. Don't use thirst as a guide, since by then it will too late. To help stay cool I wet my head with water a few minutes before the start of the race. This keeps me cooler longer. I especially do this on hot days, but sometimes I do it in colder weather of 45°F and up.

- Always give yourself plenty of time to arrive at the race. It is better to arrive too early than at the last minute and be stressed out. This can negatively affect your race performance.

- Some larger events will provide you with an electronic chip. The chip is tied through the shoelace to the outside part of one of your running shoes. The chip is used to accurately register your race finish time. Basically, it begins timing you from the moment that you go over the starting line and stops when you cross the finish line. You are asked to return the chip at the finish area. Most of my experiences with the chip have been good. In one instance a runner tripped over the chip's timing device and several hundred runners did not get timed. This was a rare exception. The chip is useful because it allows runners to get more accurate results, especially in large events when it may take several minutes to cross the starting line if you start in the back of the pack.

- When you arrive to the race warm up for a few minutes. Do it longer on cold days and shorter in hot and humid weather. Start with a short jog to loosen up your muscles and follow with some stretches. Be careful not to overdo it. The idea is to warm up without getting tired before the race. Drink plenty of water as you warm up. I usually start stretching when I wake up. For longer races over 15K, I stretch for a few minutes the night before. I believe that the race warm up should not take longer than fifteen minutes.

- Line up according to your race goals and realistic running speed. The front of the pack is where the fastest runners find their place. In most events these are runners averaging 6 and under minutes per mile. Behind the first few rows you find a mixture of slow, medium, and fast runners. If you are a beginner or don't care about your finish time choose the middle to the back of the pack. On the other hand if you have a specific time goal then try to start as close to the front as you can, but be true to yourself and others. If your average race pace is 9 minutes per mile or more then avoid the front line with the fast runners. Besides risking a fall in the front you can wear yourself out in the first quarter of a mile trying to keep up with the front runners. When the race starts, go slower during the first half mile until you reach your race pace. Sometimes this is hard since we tend to run at the pace of the pack. If the pack is not moving fast enough don't panic. Keep moving along. Soon it will open up. Avoid tiring yourself out in the first mile rush. Once you reach a steady race pace you will be able to pass other runners.

- While waiting at the start line try to relax your muscles by moving slowly in place. Running with tense muscles is more

119

difficult and slows you down. During the race check how tense your muscles are especially in the upper body area. Sometimes we are not aware of the tension in our neck and shoulders. While running relax the upper body by dropping the arms and shoulders for a moment. This will reduce the tension in that area.

• If at any moment you feel dizzy or sick please stop running immediately and seek attention from the race officials or other runners. Never risk your health for staying in the race. Your well being is always more important than running.

• Once the race starts it is important to keep hydrated especially if it is a hot day or a longer than 4 miles event. Drink water at each water station. As you approach the water station move carefully to the side without cutting off other runners right behind you. Point to the volunteer holding the water cup so that he/she knows your intentions. This will minimize the risk of accidents and will save you time. Once you get the water cup don't stop. Keep moving either running or walking to avoid causing a traffic jam. It takes practice to learn to drink water while running without choking. It is best to slow down and walk a few steps while taking a few sips of water. Once you are finished don't throw the half-filled or empty cup over your head without looking if there is someone right next to you. A couple of times I have been grazed by water cups or gotten water in my face from the runner in front. With a quick look to the side toss the cup off the road or just drop the empty cup straight down.

• After you finish the race don't sit down right away. Keep walking for several minutes to cool off. Start drinking fluids soon after.

• The post-race party begins as soon as you cross the finish line. This event is usually held right near the finish area. Here is where you have the opportunity to mingle with other runners while replenishing your body with fluids and healthy food. Most races provide water, sport drinks, bananas, oranges and some type of bread or similar item. At some events free beer is offered after the race. Although I can always enjoy a good beer, I believe this is not the best time to drink alcoholic beverages. First we need to re-hydrate our systems. Beer is a diuretic and not the type of fluid our body needs after a race. We need to replace the lost fluids and not take away more. In my opinion plain water and non-carbonated sports drinks give you the best option.

Running is a very open sport. One reason that makes races more exciting is that all runners run the race together regardless of their ability. Slow, middle of the pack, and fast runners all share the same road. It is common to see some of the world's best runners at the larger races around the country. In Jacksonville we get several top national runners at the annual 15K River Run. In what other major sport you can meet and compete with the super athletes? There isn't any that I know of, unless of course, you are a top athlete yourself. I have met several elite runners at races including Todd Williams (River Run 15K), Jeff Galloway (Disney Marathon), Bill Rodgers (NYC Marathon), John Tuttle (Running Camp), Andrey Kuznetsov (Matanzas 5K), Tom Nyariki (Charleston's Cooper River 10K), Elana Meyer (Charleston's Cooper River 10K), Cathy O'Brien (River Run 15K), and Jacksonville resident Jerry Lawson (1997 American marathon record holder).

It is a good idea to take at least one day off after the race, but depending on the race distance and your speed of recovery more days may be necessary. The time off is needed for the body and muscles to recover from the race demands. For races under 7 miles I take 1-2 days off while for longer distances I take between 2-3 days off. The best indicator to know when to resume running is to listen to your body. If you feel worn out after the race rest an extra day.

### Preparing for the 15K River Run

Running the 9.3 miles River Run course requires serious preparation, especially if you have never run this distance or have a specific time goal. The 1999 River Run was my fifth time entering this great event. This year I wanted to lower my PR of 67:11 or get close. I had finished short the previous two years by 5 and 2 minutes respectively. Three months before the 1999 River

Run I came up with a plan that included a significant amount of bridge and endurance training. By the end of the training period I had run the Jacksonville downtown bridges 24 times. I increased my weekly runs from 3-4 to 4-5 days. For speed training I participated in several races including 5K, 5M, and a half marathon during the three month period. I added speed interval training to many of my weekly runs and complemented my workouts with a series of upper body exercises. I even attended several seminars covering different areas of the runner's River Run preparation.

If you have never run the River Run, the route of the race includes two bridges: the smaller Main Street Bridge and the long steep Hart Bridge on mile 7. My bridge workouts were aimed at preparing me for the challenges of the Hart Bridge. In addition, this year I worked on downhill speed to take advantage of the bridge's descent. By the end of the three months training I felt confident that I stood a good chance to achieve my objective provided that the weather was cool on race day. I had worked hard to achieve this level of fitness and felt proud. I told myself that no matter what my finish time was I would feel that my objective was accomplished. Although I am very competitive person, running is a lot more than just a time goal. It is a continuous and self-fulfilling activity with its biggest payoff achieved every time I run. The finish time becomes less relevant when measured against the mere act of running.

The 1999 River Run turned out harder than I thought. The weather was on the warm side with the temperature in the middle 70s°F and humid. It took me 10 seconds to cross the starting line amid great effort to make my way through. The first mile was tough with hundreds of runners cutting in front. I did the first mile in 7:20, already too slow for my goal of under 67 minutes. I felt good going over the Main Street Bridge. By the time I got to the second mile I was averaging 7:25 per mile. At this point my thigh muscles started to feel tight. When I reached the third mile in 22:15 minutes I knew that a PR was out of the question. I was surprised because I had trained the bridges more than ever before. Perhaps I had overdone it. Especially my last bridge and downhill speed workout a week before the race. This was probably what affected my thigh muscles. I hadn't allowed enough time for recovery. Very tired and with thigh muscle pain I readjusted my race goal to 69 minutes. But, when I reached the 10K mark in 47 minutes I knew that 69 minutes was not feasible either. By mile seven I was thirsty and extremely tired. Tempting thoughts of walking over the Hart Bridge invaded my tired mind, but the little pride I had left kept me going. Besides I knew that if I walked my brothers would pass me. I grabbed a cup of water and took a last sip before I faced the biggest and final challenge. The Hart Bridge was grueling. When I reached the highest point I just let myself cruise down gaining all the speed I could. My legs were barely moving, and I needed all the momentum to cross the finish a mile ahead. With my last reserves almost gone I sprinted away. I knew my kids would be near the finish, so I used my last bit of energy to smile at them. I finished in 72 minutes exhausted and very sore. That day I learned a good lesson: always allow enough time for recovery before a race especially if the training has been tough and you have been putting new demands on your body.

**Race Strategy**

Whether you are racing competitively or just for fun, a race strategy is important. A race plan can help you run better. A strategy need not be a plan only to run faster but a plan to meet your race objectives. If your main goal is only to finish then a strategy can be as simple as that with a few tips to help you have a fun race. On the other hand, if you want to set a new personal record then a plan is necessary to help you achieve that goal.

As with everything there are many ways to run a race. The strategy will vary from runner to runner depending on training condition, ability, and race objective. Obviously the race plan for an elite runner will not be the same as the one for a middle of the pack runner like me. However, there are some general principles for efficient racing. A very popular strategy is to start the race slower than your normal race pace and pick up the pace as your reach the first mile or so. This allows the body to reach full potential more gently. The idea is that eventually you would reach the desired race pace and try to maintain it. When you use this strategy you should run a slower first half of the race and a faster second half. A similar concept is the one of negative splits. This consists of starting slow and running every mile a little faster until you reach your maximum race speed. This strategy is not as easy as it seems. It takes speed training and endurance to be able to run faster on every new mile when obviously your body is getting more tired as you run farther. A more extreme concept is to run the race all-out. This means go out at the fastest pace for the distance from the beginning and try to keep it up until the finish. This is what many elite runners do, but even an all-out effort requires runners to pace themselves throughout the race.

When I started racing I used to go fast from the start. Perhaps this was a habit from my track days as a sprinter. When I used the all-out strategy I would be worn out by the half mark of the race. Nevertheless, I set my 5K personal record running this way (20:17). But, I did this only for 5K races. For longer distances I usually start slower and pick up the pace later by using my watch and the mile markers as references. So, I have tried both concepts including the negative splits, and the results are mixed. For example, I haven't been able to lower my 5K record using the slower start approach nor doing negative splits. It seems that when I start out slower I can never make up the time lost in the beginning. Lately I have been experimenting in the 5K with a combination strategy of starting fast but slowing down after a few hundred yards and then increasing the speed to race pace by the first mile mark. I still haven't been able to crack my PR, but I am getting closer. So for me the all-out approach is still the most effective for distances up to 5K. The truth is that there isn't one general formula that works well for all the distances and all the events. Each race presents different conditions every time. When I set my 5K PR everything was there for this to happen. The terrain was flat, the weather was perfect in the low 50s, and I was in excellent training shape. If one of these variables had been different I wouldn't probably have run a PR that day. So when planning your race strategy take into account not only the known factors like your current running condition, type of distance, type of terrain, and expected weather conditions, but make sure to leave room for last minute adjustments caused by things beyond your control. Sometimes you can be in the best running condition and something happens on the day of the race that hinders your goal. It is just life, I guess. All you can do when this occurs is to make the best out of the experience and think that there will be other opportunities to try again.

The following are a few tips to make you race more efficiently and perhaps help you achieve your race goals.

One of the most common mistakes for many runners is to start the race too fast. They go out faster than their race pace and by the first mile or so they have used up a considerable portion of their energy. We all have made this mistake. Sometimes this can happen when we start in the front row and try to follow the fastest runners. If you start in front focus on maintaining your own pace not someone else's.

- Sometimes it is okay to start fast for the first couple of hundred yards to get away from the crowd and then settle back to a slower pace for the first mile. This is an option for competitive runners that don't want to give an inch at the start, but be careful not to keep running at the faster pace for too long and then pay later.

- If you don't want to be pulled by the fast runners, start a few yards behind the front row with the middle of the pack. This will allow you to start slower and gradually pick up your pace.

- For most non-elite runners the best strategy is to start a little slower than your intended race pace and keep this pace for the first mile. By then your muscles will be warmed up and it should be easier to settle into your race pace.

- A steady pace is the most effective way to run a race. We save energy keeping an even pace. Our body mechanics are more efficient and heat buildup is more gradual.

- If the race has uphill or downhill parts, use the strategy described in chapter 5. For uphill, slow down and lift your knees a little higher. For downhill, use the momentum of the descent to gain speed, but be careful about falling. A way to save energy is to find someone the same size or bigger and run behind him/her. This can give you 6-7% advantage because of less wind resistance. In other words let them cut the wind resistance for you. Cyclists do it all the time, but keep in mind that in some sports this is illegal.

- A good race plan is one that breaks the race into smaller sections and sets goals for each point in the race. For example, think of your desired time for each mile in the race or some other measurable breakdown. You can use the mile markers and clocks as points of reference to check if you are within target. There are many ways to do this. Having smaller goals will make it easier to attain larger ones.

- There will be some popular races with literally thousands of runners. Unless you are able to start in front, getting through the initial crowd will take several minutes. The best strategy for this is to go with the flow without trying to zigzag between runners. This will just tire you out much sooner. Be patient. Eventually the road will start to clear up.

- Visualize yourself achieving your goals in the race. For example if your goal is to finish, see yourself crossing the finish line. This can be useful when it gets tough and you feel like quitting. Use positive affirmations such as: I am a winner; I can do it; I am almost there; I am strong; It is easy; I am doing well; Today is the day; or come up with your own affirmations. This really works. Give it a try.

- During the race check your form. Shorter strides are more effective than elongated strides, which tire you sooner. Hips should be forward and loose.

- Keep in mind that body composition can play an important role in our running performance. By this I mean that our weight, height, and body build affect the way we run regardless of our training condition. For example, I am about 5'10'' and weigh 155lbs. My body build is medium. My legs are more suitable for sprinting than for long distance running, and compared to world class runners I weigh too much for my height. Some of these elite long distance runners weigh under 140lbs. On the other hand, against my brother I have an advantage. He is 6'2" and weighs 195lbs. For every step he needs to move 195lbs while I only move 155. Overall he has to work harder to complete the same distance as I. This is something to consider when evaluating your race performance.

Always put your personal safety and health first. Race smart. Don't take unnecessary risks. Remember that by running you already are a winner.

# Chapter 8 - My Favorite Races

The following sections contain a list of some favorite races in Northeast Florida and a few other places. I know that there are hundreds of wonderful races held throughout the country, but I have focused mainly on Northeast Florida events because this is where I have done most of my racing. For the races listed, I have done my best to provide accurate and current information. As a rule, I have run every race mentioned here at least once, sometimes several times. Keep in mind that the race information given here is subject to change without notice. For exact event dates and location check the race calendars available at local running stores, magazines or on the web. (Refer to Appendix-A for running publications).

## Northeast Florida Races

The number of local road races is quite large and keeps growing every year. The events vary in popularity and size. Some are small and not widely known while others have become a local tradition attracting several hundred runners each time. Every year I try to run a few new events as well as several established ones. Although I like running most of them, my favorite races are usually the smaller ones. These are usually well organized and support a good cause. Below is a description of 22 Northeast Florida races. This is not a complete list. The others are for you to discover.

## Matanzas 5K

This scenic race is held in picturesque St. Augustine, Florida during the last weekend in January. It is perhaps the largest and most popular 5K in Northeast Florida. It has been around for several years. The race starts at 9am on Castillo Drive by the baseball fields and goes through the historic section of this ancient city. Although I have never been able to break my PR in this course, the terrain is flat with lots of turns on narrow streets. The Ancient City Road Runners (ACRR) club does a great job organizing this event. A free 1-mile fun run is offered for kids. The first several hundred finishers get a tee-shirt and a ribbon. Their raffle prizes are among the best I have seen in races with expensive items such as electronics, watches, bikes, running gear, and gift certificates. This race is high on my list. I guess the opportunity to run in this lovely city is too hard to pass up.

## Winter Beaches Runs (5M & 10M)
This double race is a popular event. It is held around the middle of February in Jacksonville Beach. Both distances start together and go along the beach. This can be a tough race especially for beginners or if you are not used to running on sand. Sometimes the weather can be windy and cold or just perfect. If you like a little challenge this is a great race.  Start with the 5M if you are a beginner or have never run on sand.

## Ortega River Run 5M
This popular event is held around the 3$^{rd}$ week in February. The 5-mile course goes through scenic and shaded streets of the Ortega neighborhood including the Roosevelt Bridge on US 17. The race starts and finishes on Ortega Boulevard in front of St. Marks Episcopal School. This event offers plenty of challenge because of its length and the bridge, making it a nice stepping stone for runners training for longer distances. The post-race party is fun with lots of food and runners to mingle with. I usually enter this race as part of my speed and bridge training for the 15K River Run.

## River Run 15K
The Jacksonville 15K River Run is the largest and most well organized running event in Northeast Florida. It started in 1978 and has become a local running tradition. Every year several thousand runners gather in Jacksonville's downtown area for this popular race. The River Run is usually scheduled on the first Saturday in March. Two days prior to the 15K event a large

runner's Expo is held through race day. This is a good place to find top quality running merchandise at great prices. The River Run is a definite challenge for any runner. With two big bridges and a 9.3-mile course this race is no joke. Aside from being a tough event this is an awesome experience. The inspirational feeling of seeing thousands of runners lined up at the start make many of us want to return year after year. I have run it five times since we moved to Jacksonville in 1990. If you are a runner in Northeast Florida this is a race you don't want to miss. The post-race party is huge with lots of food and drinks for everyone. The River Run is the National 15K US Championship, which attracts several of the country's elite runners. A few years ago Todd Williams set the American record for this distance on this race. All finishers get a commemorative gift while the top 10% get a medal. If you decide to run this race you will need to prepare for the bridges, especially for the long and steep Hart Bridge. An effective workout is to run the loop of the Acosta and Main Street bridges in downtown Jacksonville several times prior to the race. In addition to the 15K event, the River Run has a 5K walk and a 1-mile fun run for kids. All of these just add to make this a wonderful running event with something for everyone.

Twilight Lighthouse 5K
This traditional 5K is held one week after the 15K River Run at the St. Augustine Lighthouse. The race course is flat and fast providing an excellent setting for a PR. The race is in the late afternoon and starts/ finishes in front of the lighthouse museum building. There is a 1-mile fun run held right after the 5K event. The post-race party is very entertaining with a live band, good food, sport drinks and free beer for all participants. Additionally, all runners can climb the over 100 steps to the top of the lighthouse at no charge. The view up there is awesome. This is a great race to enter if you have completed the River Run the week before. With that kind of preparation this should be easy. I enjoy this race because it is in the early evening so I get to sleep longer and I'm usually in great shape to break my PR. Besides St. Augustine is always nice in the evening and this race gives us a good reason to drive to this lovely city.

## Navy Run 10K

This 10K race is held during the first part of April at the Naval Air Station base in Jacksonville. It is one of the oldest events in the area dating back to 1979. Several hundred runners enter this race every year. The course is fast, flat and shaded in some parts. It offers a great opportunity to set a PR. The race is well organized including the post-race party, which has lots of food and drinks. In addition the Navy Exchange store runs a great sale of running gear right after the race. This is located near the finish area. I like this event and have run it several times in recent years. This is where I set my 10K PR of 43:29. Whether you are looking for a fast 10K or a fun time this race offers both.

## Catfish 5K

This event is the kickoff of the annual Catfish Festival held during the first week of April in Crescent City. The race starts and finishes in the center of town. The course is mostly flat with some steep grades through the nearby residential streets. After the race there are several activities taking place like the arts & crafts show, live music, and a parade along the main streets. The combination of 5K run and festival make this event a great day trip for the family. When I ran this race my whole family came along. After the race we ate brunch at a nearby coffee shop that looked like it hadn't change since the 50's. The food was excellent and the atmosphere was authentically old fashioned. We ended the morning at the arts & crafts show. Everyone had a good time.

## Run to the Sun 8K

This popular Florida Striders event is held around the middle of April in Orange Park. The race starts in front of the Kennel Club and goes south on US 17 and then turns back through River Road to finish behind the club. The course is flat, fast, and mostly shaded. This race has a clydesdale category for men and women over 200 and 150 lbs respectively. The post-race party is very complete and fun. The Florida Striders generally do a great job hosting their events and this one is no exception. I like this race because in April the weather is still nice and I get a chance to run something longer than a 5K but less than 10K. This is a good practice for anyone training for a 10K.

## Mug Run 5000

This race is held in Palatka on the first weekend in May on the same day of the Mug Race sailboat event. The race starts about three blocks from the Memorial Bridge next to the St. John's river and the public boat dock. The race starts early so you may need to allow extra time for the drive to this beautiful Florida town. The course is scenic and quite challenging going up the bridge on US 17 and over the St. John's river and back the same way. This means that about half of the race is over the big bridge. The atmosphere of the race is laid back and relaxed. The volunteers are very friendly and helpful. The post-race party includes good food, prizes, and nice awards for the winners. If you want a challenging event and a change of scenery give this a try. The sailboat race starts right after the start of the 5K. When I ran this event after the awards we watched the sailboats for a while and then went for brunch at Angels Diner, a local landmark. Palatka is a very picturesque town so this race gives us a good reason to visit this quaint area of Northeast Florida.

## Bridge to Bridge 5K

This spring race is usually held during the first week of May. The course goes over two of Jacksonville's downtown bridges providing an excellent hill-like workout. This is definitely a tough race, especially going up the steep Acosta Bridge. If you are looking for a little more challenge try this one sometime. The view of the St. John's River and downtown skyline is worth the effort.

## Memorial Day 5K

This traditional 5K event is held every year on Memorial Day in Green Cove Springs. The race is part of the Memorial Day Festival at Spring Park. The course is flat and fast. The race starts and finishes by the park. Being one of the Florida Striders events, this 5K attracts several hundred runners. There is a clydesdale division for big runners which is a nice thing. The first time my wife ran this race she was given a finisher medal for being her first race. I thought that was a great way to encourage new runners to keep running. The post-race party and awards ceremony are held at the park. I like racing early on holidays. It gets me out the door before noon and I feel energized all day. Whenever I enter this event I bring my family along and we stay for the festival activities after the race. If you are looking for a family event on Memorial Day and a good race consider this 5K.

## Run for the Pies 5K

This is a very popular evening event. The Run for the Pies 5K is held during the first half of June. The course is flat and fast and starts at the Jacksonville Landing in downtown. There are two heats, an invitational 5K for elite runners and the open event for everyone else. All men and women finishing under 20 and 24 minutes respectively, get a free pie. The post-race party is at the Jacksonville Landing. There is live music, food and drinks including beer, and free prizes. I have run this race many times and it has always been hot and humid. But it is still a great event. I keep going back every June. What better way to spend a Saturday evening than running through downtown with hundreds of runners and celebrating later by the St. John's River.

## Bridge of Lions 5K

This popular evening race is held around the third week in July in beautiful St. Augustine. The race starts by the historic Castillo de San Marcos and goes over the Bridge of Lions and continues through residential streets to finish by the bridge. This event attracts over a thousand runners every year making it one of the largest 5Ks in Northeast Florida. The post-race party is at the finish area, but the awards ceremony is usually on the other side of the bridge by the Old Market square. I really like this race. It has a special attraction that keeps me going back year after year. Perhaps it is the feeling of being there, in front of the 17th century Castillo de San Marcos sharing the warm summer evening with hundreds of runners and friends. Perhaps it is because this was the first race I did in Florida and it reminds me of where I started and how far I have come as runner. I guess you get my point. This is a great race. Besides, there is a big controversy about the future of the Bridge of Lions, which could affect the future of this event. There is an effort to replace the bridge to improve the flow of traffic but many people oppose it since this bridge is part of the history of St. Augustine. I hope that a compromise can be found for both sides, but in the meantime I will continue to enter this race every year.

## Tour de Pain

This is a unique event in Northeast Florida, three races in 24 hours. Held during the first half of August this challenging trio is made to test your endurance. The first race is a 4-mile run on the beach and it takes place on Friday evening. The second race is a 1-mile run on the road. This takes place Saturday morning. The third and final race is a 5K road run held in the evening of Saturday. All finishers of the three events get a medal, but you don't have to enter all three races to participate. Each event can be entered separately. I have run this series of races twice and they were definitely tough. By the time you are done with the third event you will be glad the 'pain' is over. Overall, I like the challenges offered by these races. If you want to test your will and endurance, the Tour de Pain provides just that.

## Run for Fun Olympics 5K

These are a series of weekly 5K events held at the Florida Community College at Jacksonville's North Campus in the months of August through October. Every Tuesday evening at 6:30pm a 5K race is held. The course is a mixture of wooded trail and sidewalk around the campus. There is a small fee required to enter each event. There are tee-shirts and ribbons for all age group winners, which due to the reduced number of entrants is usually everybody. There is no post-race party but there are water fountains. The adjacent locker room facilities are open for runners after the race. If you are looking for a fun but effective workout try this one. I like this series of races because they are simple and hassle free. Basically you go, pay, run, and you're done. Plus they can easily be a substitute for speed workouts.

## Summer Beach Run 5M

This summer evening race is held at Jacksonville Beach in late August. This is a popular event especially among hardcore runners. The combination of hot humid weather and the 5-mile beach course make this race usually tough. I remember running one year when the humidity was high, the temperature was around 90°F plus, and there was no sea breeze. The result was that we were about to pass out. Runners were throwing up and some were just walking back. This can definitely be a challenging feat. On the other hand beach runs tend to inspire me and this is a nice event.

The runners, the beach, and the race make it a magical evening. The post-race party is great with lots of food and drinks to celebrate the hard work. If you have never run this race you may want to give it a try, but go slow the first time.

## Autumm Fitness 5K
This traditional race is hosted by the Florida Striders Track Club. It is held during the first half of September in front of the Kennel Club in Orange Park. The course is fast and very similar to the Run to the Sun 8K except shorter. Like other Striders events this one has a clydesdale category for big runners. There is also a 1-mile fun run right after the 5K. All fun run finishers get a ribbon. This is a good reason to bring kids along and encourage them to participate and have some fun too. Whenever I am looking for a fast 5K this is one of my favorite ones.

## Race for the Cure 5K
This event is held during the first half of October in Jacksonville Beach. Its proceeds benefit breast cancer research at the local and national level. There are two 5K heats, one for men and one for women. The race starts and finishes by the Seawalk Pavilion. The course is flat, fast, and on pavement. The event draws a significant number of runners, especially women. There is a small informational expo after the race. The post-race activities are very inspiring as breast cancer survivors are recognized by the organizers. I try to run this race every year because it supports such an important cause. Plus it is much fun to be there in the front line with my fellow runners. The food is good, too.

## Corporate Cup 5K
This weekday evening event is held around the second week of October at The Jacksonville Landing. It is geared for employees of companies, businesses, and government agencies. To enter the race you must be at least a part-time employee. The companies must enter their runners in one or more teams in one of several divisions according to type of business. In addition, teams are allowed from running and health clubs, but they must enter under the club division. The course is flat and fast. The post-race party has live music and good food. It is a nice opportunity to mingle with runners from just about every local business around town. This event is very popular among local companies. Several hundred

runners run it every year. If you get the opportunity to run this race, do it. It is a way to participate in a fun race while encouraging your company or business to support running.

Mandarin Run 10K

This popular event is held during the first week of November in Mandarin. The race starts and finishes at Mandarin Park. The course is flat, mostly shaded and fast. This is great event to set a PR. There is a fun run for kids and families after the main race. The post-race party takes place at the park, so there is plenty of room for mingling with family and friends. Plus, the kids can run around freely or play on the nearby playground. I have always enjoyed running along the shaded streets of Mandarin, and this race gives me a chance to do just that. If you are looking for a fast 10K course consider this one.

Outback ½ Marathon

This race is held on Thanksgiving Day in the Mandarin area of Jacksonville. The course is flat, fast and mostly shaded going through residential streets west of San Jose Boulevard. In recent years this event has become a classic of Northeast Florida. Several hundred runners show up every year for the 13.1 mile run. The race is well organized and the post-event party is great. I like this race because it serves me as preparation for the winter season. Plus, in late November the weather is usually cooler, which I really enjoy. A portion of the race proceeds is donated to the local food bank. So this is another good reason to enter this event, especially being on Thanksgiving Day. If you have any plans to run a marathon some day this is definitely a race to consider since this is only half the distance you will have to cover in a full marathon.

Jacksonville Marathon

This traditional race is held between the second and third week in December. This event consists of three races: the marathon, a half marathon, and a 5K. All races start in front of Bolles School in San Jose Boulevard. The marathon and half marathon start about an hour earlier than the 5K. The marathon and half marathon course is mostly shaded and flat. The 5K course goes over the final miles of the marathon course. All three events combined attract several hundred runners each year, many being from out of town because the Jacksonville Marathon is one of the last marathons to qualify for the upcoming Boston Marathon. Although I have not run this marathon yet, I have done the 5K several times. All three races finish at the Bolles School track. The whole event is fun and the food is good for everyone. The post-race party doesn't end at the finish, and there is usually a celebration party held in the evening at one of the local hotels. I like this race because the weather is often cool, and it is a healthy way to stay in shape for the end of year holidays.

Many local races have a 1-mile fun run for kids following the main event. These are free for the most part. But you may still be required to fill out an entry form for insurance purposes. I like these events because they provide a wonderful opportunity to get the family involved in running. Many times I bring my kids along so that they can enter the fun run. They love running especially if my wife or I run with them. Most fun runs give out ribbons to all finishers. Since each event is different the best thing is to check the race information to see if they will have a fun run.

## A Word of Thanks

Organizing a road race is not simple, nor cheap. There are many expenses required to make sure things go smoothly. For example, insurance for the runners, hiring local police officers to keep the event safe, closing public roads, getting the portable bathrooms, buying awards, getting drinks and food, and paying the race organizers for the setup, just to name a few. The point I am trying to make is that as runners we usually see only the final product and sometimes don't think of all the coordination and effort it took for the race to take place. There are many people behind each event ranging from the race director, race staff, medical personnel and many volunteers. We need to thank them all because without them most races would not be possible. In addition let's not forget the sponsors since they are footing most of the cost of the races, which helps to keep entry fees low. So next time you go to a race remember to thank the people working there, and make it a point to support the sponsors by choosing their products and services whenever you can. At some point you may want to volunteer at a race to see things from the other side. It is fun and you will better appreciate the work these people do for us.

## Some Great Out of Town Races

There are hundreds of out of town races held every year. If you are interested in events outside Northeast Florida there are multiple race calendars available through the internet, running magazines, and local running stores. Check Appendix-A for specific publication names and more information. During my years running the roads I have made it a point to enter several out of town events. It is an easy way to combine running and leisure time. The following is a sample of the five out of town races I enjoyed the most. My intention is not to endorse any of these but mainly to share my experience in racing out of our area. Perhaps this is something that you have been thinking of doing as well.

Disney ½ Marathon
This event is part of the Disney Marathon held in early January at the Magic Kingdom in Orlando, Florida. This is a fairly new race, but it has gained popularity every year. It is well organized, and for all Disney lovers it offers the unique opportunity to run through the world famous theme parks. Both the marathon and half marathon start together before dawn from the parking lot at Epcot. The race goes through the parks and around them. Half marathoners finish at the Magic Kingdom. In 1999 I ran this race with my brother. Only 9000 marathoners and 4000 half marathoners were allowed to register. The whole experience was great fun. We got up at 3:30 in the morning to arrive at 4:30am at the Epcot parking lot as had been suggested by the organizers. If you decide to run this race try to get plenty of sleep the week prior since you may not get much the night before. When we got to the race area there was not much time to hang around. By 5am we were on our way to the starting area which was about a mile away. Everyone got in their respective corrals according to their numbers. We moved to the first row of our staging area and waited there. When the race started at 6:00am it was still dark and a bit cool. It took us a couple of minutes to cross the starting line and a few more to get into a steady pace. The course was mostly flat with several turns and some overpasses over the road around the theme parks. After the 9th mile I was suffering knee pain and was really hoping to see the finish line. No such luck but when I reached mile 12 in agony only one thought crossed my mind, how lucky I was to be doing only the half marathon. I couldn't help but smile knowing that I had just one more mile to

go while many fellow runners were just beginning the second half of the full marathon. As soon as we crossed the finish a blanket and a medal were handed out. We returned the timing chips and went to get food. The food and drinks were given out as we exited the finish area. Once out we had to walk to the bus area to get a ride back to the start. I liked this event except that I wish that the finish area were better. I just felt that we were rushed out and there was not much time to hang out with other runners. Everything else I enjoyed. If you decide to enter this race send your entry early since they fill up quickly. Tip: Make sure to put your estimated finish time on your application when you send it. They will assign you a starting corral depending on the time you submit. I made the mistake to write down a slow time, and they assigned me to a slower corral, so it cost me a few minutes at the beginning of the race.

## Tybee Island 5K

This 5K is held along with a marathon and half marathon on Tybee Island, Georgia around the second week in February. Tybee Island is a beautiful coastal community located outside Savannah. The marathon and half marathon start a few minutes before the 5K. The course is flat and fast around the island. When I ran this event several hundred runners entered the races. The weather was cool and ideal for a fast time. My family and I had arrived the previous night and stayed at one of the hotels nearby. The people were very friendly and laid back. After the run we toured the island and visited the historic Tybee Island Lighthouse. Later we ate lunch in Savannah and walked around the historic center, a charming area full of shops and restaurants. Being only 2 ½ hours from Jacksonville this was a nice option for a fun weekend getaway combining the race with quality family time.

## Tri-State 5K

This race is held in April in Gainesville, Florida. The 5K event is part of three races starting together: a 5K, a 10K, and a 15K. The course is a flat 5K loop, so depending on which distance you enter you go once, twice or three times around. Although this is a fairly new event it is very well organized. Runners are provided a timing chip for accuracy. The races start and finish in the center of town of the Haile Plantation. Last year when I ran this race the weather was great for running, a clear sky and 50°F. We left Jacksonville at 6am and arrived around 7:40. A little too close for me but still enough time for a quick warm up and getting to the starting line. Usually, I run faster in cool weather, so I finished in 20:38, my best time that year. After the 5K there was a 2-mile fun run that my wife decided to enter at the last minute. She enjoyed it. The post-race party was better than many I have seen. The food was good and plentiful. After filling our tummies we watched the awards ceremony at the nearby square. Here they had several activities for kids including a magician that we all enjoyed. We left around noon and decided to have lunch in Gainesville before driving home. Overall this was a nice event for the whole family. We added it to our list of day trip race getaways.

Cooper River Bridge Run 10K
This race is held in Charleston, South Carolina at the end of March or beginning of April. This is one of the largest 10Ks in the United States bringing thousands of runners each year. The course is very challenging with two big steep bridges between miles 1 and 4. The race starts in Mt. Pleasant and finishes in downtown Charleston. A big expo and pasta dinner are held the day before. As in most major events a chip is provided to each runner for accurate timing results. The post-race party is held at Marion Square. Last year my brother Rod and I joined several Jacksonville Track Club runners going to this race. The JTC chartered a bus for the trip. We left the day before the event at 1pm and arrived in Charleston around 6pm. After picking up our race packets we decided to stay for the pasta dinner. It was good, and we were hungry so we got seconds. The next morning we met the other runners at 6:30am to go to the race site. When we arrived at the starting area we saw thousands of runners already there. After a few minutes of warm up we entered the staging area. I had a seeded number, first one ever, and we found a place right behind the elite group. Promptly at 8am Bill Murray, the actor, fired the gun and 13,000 runners took off. I was glad to be near the front. I reached the 1st mile in 7 minutes and started the ascent of the first bridge. It was tough especially because we were running against a strong breeze. Once I reached the top of the first bridge I realized that the suffering was far from over. There it was, the second bridge, less than half a mile away. Going up this time felt harder. I was getting tired. Finally at mile

four I reached downtown, from there flat land until the finish. Running more on will power than on energy, I completed the race in 45:29. I was very happy with this performance, and the fact that I beat my brother by over a minute. After the race we hung out by the food for a while and enjoyed the sunny and cool morning. Marion Square was packed with runners. Before walking back to the bus we met the race winners and took a picture with them. On the ride back we slept, a well deserved rest. I really enjoyed this race because it offered something for everyone. I liked the challenge of the course and the historic setting. Plus it was a chance to visit Charleston, a place I had never been before. This is a great race. If you are interested in a well organized and big league 10K try this one.

New York City Marathon

This world class event takes place every year in early November. Since 1970 the New York Marathon has been one of the world's most popular marathons. Today over 30,000 runners enter this great race each year. The 26.2-mile course is challenging covering New York City's five boroughs and including several bridges. The marathon celebration begins the day before at the runner's expo. It continues with the free pasta dinner at the Tavern on the Green restaurant in Central Park. The dinner is excellent and a perfect opportunity to meet other runners. Very early on race day free buses begin shuttling runners from midtown Manhattan to the starting area by the Verrazano-Narrows Bridge on Staten Island. The bus ride is under an hour. The marathon finishes in Central Park by the Tavern on the Green. There are water and first aid stations, and toilets throughout the marathon course. Along the course there are bands playing live music and literally thousands of spectators cheering runners on. All finishers get a commemorative medal. The awards ceremony is held later at a nearby hotel. There is a celebration party later in the evening for all runners and their guests. As you can see there are plenty of activities before and after the marathon. When I ran this race in 1996 I was not sure what to expect. I had been training physically and mentally for several months, yet I still felt a little unprepared. I traveled to New York by train from Jacksonville. The trip was very interesting, but more exhausting than I had anticipated. Although I got there a day before, I was a bit worn out. Initially I'd planned to rest upon arrival at the hotel, but with the excitement of the race I couldn't force myself to stay in my room. Standing in line to get my race packet I realized I was in New York City and only a few hours before this huge event. There were runners from all around the world, all ages and shapes. In general people were very friendly, and since we were all there for the same reason it was easy to feel at home. The expo was enormous, perhaps twice the size of our River Run expo. Later than evening I attended the pasta dinner. This was free for all runners. Because of the number of people we were given a specific time for dinner. The food was top-notch. I forced myself not to overeat, but it wasn't easy with so much there for us to take. That night I had trouble sleeping, but I was ready. By 6:15am I was jogging from the hotel to the bus pick up. This served as my warm up. The morning was cool, in the low 40's with a clear sky. The bus ride was a 'trip'. There was no bathroom and some runners were in desperate need of one. The driver couldn't do much. Seeing one guy pace front to back was making everyone else anxious. Finally after 45 minutes we arrived at the start area. This was an awesome sight, thousands of runners crammed in an area next to the Verrazano bridge. I saw some European runners change their shorts right in the open in front of everyone — No bashfulness in the old continent. By 10:30 I was waiting in the starting corral assigned to me. Promptly at 10:50 the gun went off. All I could see was a gigantic mass of people moving slowly up the bridge. Everywhere I looked there were literally thousands of runners moving in the same direction. It took me almost two miles to get in the clear. By mile 3, I was keeping a slow but steady pace. My race goal was to finish without walking. I had brought a disposable camera with me to record this memorable event. One of the things that pleased me the most was seeing the spectators cheering us on. They were everywhere along the road. When I crossed into Manhattan after mile 15, I felt like a world class runner. Here the people were literally shouting at us for our effort. It was a very special feeling. A similar thing I felt entering Central Park around mile 23. All along the park there were cheering spectators. By this point I needed their encouragement because I had nothing left. Looking back, the last mile was probably the hardest of all because I was physically worn out and mentally I was counting every step to the finish line. After I crossed the finish I went to the first aid tent. I was okay but needed a warm drink. I got a hot chocolate and walked back to the hotel. Later that evening I walked to a nearby restaurant to replenish myself. I felt I deserved it. After dinner I went to the celebration party for an hour. That night I wore my medal everywhere. I had earned it. The next morning I got up late and well rested. I checked out and had a big breakfast before heading back to the train station for the trip home. For the next several days I walked like I had ridden the mechanical bull. This is a fantastic event. It never ceases to amaze me that they can close half of the Verrazano Bridge and many major roads in a mega city like New York for this race. It is just hard to believe. I really commend the organizers and hundreds of volunteers for a first class event. Just imagine the coordination needed to host a race of this nature and size. I have never been to a better event than the New York City Marathon. The experience is unbelievable. I plan to return someday with my wife. In my opinion every serious runner should run New York at least once. For more information contact the New York Road Runners Club.

Getting ready to start.

The thrill of another race.

In the chute remember to stay in line and tear off your tag.

Feeling great after 13.1 miles.

Jacksonville's Main Street Bridge, part of the 15K River Run course.

The Hart Bridge, high above the St. Johns River, is the 15K River Run's toughest challenge.

# Part Four: *Running Spirit*

---

"The longer I run, the more I learn about myself."

# Chapter 9 - Keep on Running

## Inspire Others

A good way to stay motivated is to be an inspiration to other people. Every runner can do this by sharing his experiences with family and friends. Most runners tend to be introverted people, so openness is not our biggest strength. We enjoy solitude and run for our own reasons. This is fine, but life is more meaningful when we give and share our experiences with other human beings. What a great opportunity we runners have to take an active role in influencing others to get involved in fitness. In other words, lead by example and become an ambassador of running. We run because we love it and have already seen many of its advantages, so why not share our running experience with friends and loved ones? Use this knowledge to positively motivate others to become active and find out for themselves.

In recent years we have seen a big increase in the number of people involved in fitness, but the percent of the total population is still small. The fitness campaign of the last twenty years has yet to motivate the large majority of people. I believe we can make a bigger impact if each runner makes a personal goal to get another person involved in a regular running program. Because we have a more lasting influence on our families and friends than the media or government do, the results of this effort would quickly show the positive effects. The number of new runners could grow dramatically.

Several years ago I asked my two younger brothers to run with me. For a while we trained together and competed in several local races. Although today they do not run as much as I do, they too have made running part of their busy lifestyles. Every year we run in several local races where we test our running strength against each other. Last year I convinced my wife to start jogging. She has been doing it regularly since and has run a few road races. From not being able to jog even a mile she can now run two hours without stopping. She recently completed her first 15K Gate River Run in less than two hours. A friend of my wife's, who hadn't run since high school started running with her. My brother's fiancée started running about one year ago motivated mainly by him. The point is that one person influences another, and the chain goes on, and by motivating others we keep ourselves motivated too. It can be contagious and a win-win situation for everyone involved.

**Motivate Yourself**

When inspiration alone is not enough to keep you running there are several other things you can do to stay motivated. Read books or magazines about running. Subscribe to running newsletters, or watch running movies. Another simple thing is to have a picture taken of you running and put it in a visible place. This will be a powerful reminder that you are a runner. It may be easier to stay motivated if you hang around with runners. For example join a running club, make running friends, or sign up for a race. For more ideas, read the last section of chapter 4.

A while back during a two-week overseas vacation I cut my running to one third of the usual. As soon as I got back home I had to leave on a business trip so my training did not get any better. After over a month lost I started increasing my runs to the normal level. At first it was difficult since I was feeling slow and heavy on my legs. I had gained a few pounds and was less motivated to run. It was as if an invisible force of laziness was taken over me. I forced myself to do my runs. I picked up a few running magazines, visited the local running store and signed up for a race. Slowly I started to regain my running interest. With every new run I felt lighter and my legs gained more power. As I was doing a long run one night I remember listening to the sounds of the crickets, frogs, and night birds, and thinking how much others were missing by not being out here experiencing the wonders of nature that night.

Sometimes the day before a race I watch a running movie. There are a few available at the video stores. Watching these movies gives me the inspiration I need for the race. I get psyched up. A few months ago I rented the movie "Without Limits", which tells the story of the late running legend Steve Prefontaine. I really wanted to watch this movie so I was the first person to check out the video at my local store. Watching Steve Prefontaine's all-out running style was all I needed to get inspired for my local race that weekend. But regardless of all the advice I can give you, it is ultimately you who must learn to keep yourself motivated. There is no magic formula. If you don't do your part you will lose interest. Think of all the valuable benefits you get from running and make them good reasons to keep you going. Be creative and use your imagination to come up with ideas to help you stay active. If you truly enjoy running keep doing it.

## Commitment is the Key

Your motivation to run will be a lot stronger and long lasting when there is commitment and discipline behind it. When you make the commitment to run and appreciate the benefits of this activity, staying motivated will be much easier. Discipline is what keeps things glued together. It takes discipline to keep your commitment alive, and discipline will provide the order needed to keep your running program manageable. Without these qualities you may eventually lose interest. But together, they create a strong base to guarantee the long-term success of your running program.

Many times throughout my running years I have felt tired and ready to quit. Two things have kept me going, my strong commitment to a fit life, and the inner peace I experience from running. Remember that running is less of a destination and more of a journey. It is an activity that you do time after time with no end in sight. Make running an important priority in your life. Make it a habit. Ultimately, to succeed running must become second nature. My vision is that someday when the majority of people practice exercise regularly, the world will be a better place. A fitter world will turn into a more peaceful society. As a consequence many of today's endemic social problems such as violence, stress, broken relationships, and poor health should decrease.

# Chapter 10 - The Complete Runner

People run for many different reasons. Some days, I feel like a new runner enjoying the discovery of new routes and emotions. Other times I am driven by the spark of competition as I prepare for an upcoming race. Yet, most days, I just run to feel free and leave my worries behind. We are complex beings with ever-changing preferences and motivations for doing what we do. In the early stages of running we thrive on the discovery of new feelings and the experience of running. With time we realize that this is more than just pure physical effort. We sense that running has much more to offer. We want to reach higher and move beyond the physical aspect.

Sometimes it seems that we pay too much attention to our body conditioning and forget our inner selves. If you think about it, we are amazing beings, a unique combination of tangible and intangible. Staying fit needs to involve all aspects of ourselves, a total fitness approach. Running can help us open the mind and nourish the spirit. It can be the springboard for a journey of self-discovery and positive thinking. Over the years my running has evolved. The spiritual calm I get from my workout is a big factor that keeps me coming back. Through running I experience all parts of me. I would not be a complete runner without nurturing the unseen side of myself: the parts that I cannot touch but I know are always present, my mind and spirit. As my legs take me forward my mind is soaring. Thoughts come and go. I feel lighter, as if floating with the rhythm of my stride. New ideas arise, and my body, mind, and spirit become one.

## A Positive Mind

If you think you can, you are right. If you think you can't, you are right. I believe this statement is true. We are mainly what we believe we are capable of. That's because our mind is very powerful, and it is always working to make us be the way we see ourselves. Imagine what would happen if we used the mind positively to help us achieve our goals. Our lives would improve tremendously, but the first thing is to believe that this is possible, that we have the power to influence our life. Positive thinking helps us unleash this power. For some reason most of us ignore this way of looking at life. Usually we see the glass half empty instead of half full. Perhaps this is because we are so used to thinking negatively or being doubtful. But, it doesn't need to be like that, we always have the choice to think positively and see the good side of everything.

When we look at things positively our whole outlook on life changes. It works like magic. Have you ever expected negative things to see them actually happen? On the other hand, have you ever expected a good outcome to see it materialize later? I believe that a lot of the events in our life are greatly influenced by the way we think, either positively or negatively. A positive mind acts like a magnet attracting positive things to our lives. In the past when I met someone that was always happy I thought that this person was putting an act. How could someone always be feeling upbeat? The answer is by having a positive attitude towards life. By being positive we show confidence in ourselves.

It is my belief that we are not in this world by accident. Life is too perfectly engineered to be a random event. We have a purpose, and a way to discover this is by opening our mind. A positive mind is an open mind, and shows a winning attitude. A negative mind is a closed mind, and reflects limitation. Negative thinking brings fear, doubt, and worry into our lives. Obviously life is not perfect, so there will be times when things don't go the way we want. The important thing is to learn from every experience and keep an optimistic outlook. Things will eventually always improve. Worrying is a waste of precious energy. There is no sense in getting frustrated about things that may never happen or that we don't have any control over. Positive thinking reduces feelings like fear, doubt, and worry. Running is a positive activity. It brings good things to our lives. With a positive attitude running will be much more enjoyable. It is smart to be positive. I must admit that I haven't always been a positive person. Being a critical individual I many times see the glass half-empty. Running has helped me improve my outlook on life. Because it makes me feel good about myself, the positive side of things stands out more clearly. How can I feel negative during an early morning run along the beautiful Florida beaches? The point is that no matter how bad a day I may be having, after running I always feel happy and positive.

## Meditation

We live in a fast-paced changing world. We seem to have more stressful lives than our ancestors ever did. But, if we look at history people have always had stressful events in their lives. It is part of life. The difference is that today people spend very little time relaxing. We never stop to breathe a moment of peace. Our ancestors had many stressing events too, but they lived life at a slower pace, which allowed them to relax more often. We can reduce much of the stress in our lives by slowing down, exercising, and practicing a little relaxation. As runners it is a good habit to include a few minutes of relaxation or meditation into your weekly schedule. There are several forms of meditation available. If you have never done this before get a book at your local library or bookstore. A better alternative is to attend a relaxation class offered at local schools and fitness centers. Look up the community education course offerings in your area. Some companies offer Yoga, Tai Chi, and other meditation classes as part of wellness benefits to their employees. Adding a few minutes of relaxation to your daily schedule will cut down your stress level and make you feel better.

Several years ago, I learned meditation techniques when I was going through some stressful events in my life. Now, I meditate regularly throughout the week. This practice helps me to relax and retune myself after the stresses of the day. It is a needed peaceful moment. It makes me feel more relaxed and positive. When meditating I prefer to lie down in a quiet and private place, usually my bedroom floor. I close my eyes and begin relaxing every muscle of my body. Sometimes I can feel the tension of muscles around my jaw, neck, or arms. I tell my body to let go of all tension and relax my breathing. I visualize that every breath out releases tension, and every breath in fills me with peace. It may seem odd at first, but you will get used to it quickly. While I am meditating I let my mind drift from place to place without trying to force any thoughts. I do this for ten or fifteen minutes and then I slowly regain control of my muscles and sit up. The feeling of peace and relaxation lasts for hours. I usually do this in the evening. Many of the world-class athletes practice relaxation as part of their training routine. If you are not already meditating on a regular basis, try it out for a week. It is likely to enhance the peacefulness you get from running and reduce the unwanted stress. The best part of all is that it is simple to learn and free. Choose a relaxation technique and make it part of your running experience.

## The Path of Pennies

Life is a wonderful mystery. In this amazing journey we are constantly searching for answers and purpose. The more we search the more questions we have. Sometimes it seems as if one of our main objectives is to keep searching and asking.

Through running my spirituality has been enriched tremendously. It is as if God has found a way to communicate with me and I have welcomed God into my life. It wasn't always like this. I was baptized Catholic and attended a very orthodox Catholic school. Although my family was less religious, at school I learned about an authoritative God with infinite power and wisdom, but with very high demands for our salvation. This more than anything made me fear God. As a young boy it didn't make sense, why would God be so strict and show so little understanding. I slowly began to distance myself from religion. I maintained a passive relationship with God going to Church only a few times per year, perhaps more out of fear than belief. When I started running in my late 20s it was like a spark ignited inside me. I felt more connected with the surrounding nature and the universe. It was as if a little window had opened to a Supreme Being. Running helped me find God again. But this time I held a different view of God. This was a loving, understanding and positive God, a God less demanding and authoritative. A God inspiring total love and trust, not fear. Today, I am a strong believer in God, the Supreme Being of

Energy behind all creation in the universe. We are all part of this Divine Energy. You can see God's signature everywhere. All you need to do is start noticing.

Over a year ago I began finding pennies and other coins along my path. Yes, coins like pennies, nickels, dimes, and quarters. At first I thought it was just a coincidence, but it seemed to happen very often. I was finding them along the streets, sidewalks, parking lots, buildings, stores, and some very unusual places. It was like whenever I wasn't looking I found one. This experience has been going on steadily since then. Many times, I have tried to consciously find a coin but I never see any, while I can be walking and suddenly look down at my side to see the coin right there, as if it were staring at me. I believe this is a form of communication between God and me. I feel very privileged that God has chosen this way to acknowledge me with these coins. Receiving these coins has made me realize all the blessings in my life. Many times we take our loved ones, our health, and our happiness for granted. These coins have become symbolic reminders of the real gifts I have to be thankful for. Now, I remember to be a little nicer to someone or more forgiving as a way of thanking God for His blessings. In the beginning when this experience first started to take place I was curious. I didn't know what to make of this until I heard that other people were having similar experiences with the coins. I believe that God chooses different ways to communicate with us and this is just one of them.

Now you know this secret. I share this so that you see that running is much more than a simple sport. I believe running enables the process of self-discovery and spirituality because it removes many of the artificial layers we are so accustomed to carry with us. When we run, it is just we alone, moving by our own effort, without the distractions of social interaction. Running opens our souls to the universe, to God. I use my daily runs to communicate with God and to ask for guidance. God said in the Bible, ask and it will be given. I believe it really works. All we need to do is ask from our heart. Life is much more meaningful when we develop a close relationship with God. Open your heart to God. Ask God to lead you. Look for the signs. If you trust Him, He will lead you to the right path. Someone may think that this has nothing to do with running but it does. I believe running brings us a step closer to our soul. We begin seeing ourselves in a more natural state. We begin seeing the hand of God in everything. For many people running becomes a transformation.

As I completed my training run tonight I stopped to admire the clear sky. Thousands of stars shimmering above reminding us that we are not alone, that we are part of a whole. So many unknown worlds out there waiting to be understood by future generations. How far we have come in so little time and yet how much we don't know about our own existence. I feel humbled by the immensity of the universe, but happy to be alive and part of it. I feel fortunate for this moment watching the stars in the cold night. But most importantly, I feel blessed to be able to share my life with my family. Many of us keep busy lifestyles that make it easy to lose sight of what is really important in life. Running helps me put things back in perspective. It acts as my life compass. How lucky we are each day of our lives. Every moment is precious, every run is unique and there will never be one exactly like that again. Life is a gift full of wonderful emotions and experiences like the innocent smile of a child or the unconditional love of animals. Life is tough and fragile at the same time. One moment we are here, the next we are gone - A mystery like many we find on this journey. But mysteries are good. They keep us seeking for answers. I thank God for every new day, every new moment, and every new run.

## A Free Spirit

Up to this point I have suggested that you set goals for your running, keep a running log, track the miles of your shoes, and time yourself as a way to measure your improvements. This is all fine and very useful, especially as a beginner, since it will give you order and keep you focused. But this is not what running is all about. It is much more.

After years of continuous running I have seen a big change in myself. Initially running was exciting because I was discovering its many immediate benefits. I enjoyed participating in races and trained mainly to improve my times. I kept detailed running logs and timed myself in every run. All of this was a great experience, and it got me hooked on running. But at some point I started to care less about my race times and more about enjoying each run.

In other aspects of my life I reevaluated my goals and came to terms with what is really important to me. This transformation helped me discover a hidden part of me that had been within me all along, my inner self. This may sound a little strange if you have not experienced it but for me it is very real. I still keep a log and enjoy running races, but these are not the main objectives anymore. Perhaps I am becoming less of a competitor and more of a runner.

The other day I went on an afternoon run when it started to pour rain. I loved it. A few minutes later I was soaking wet, but I felt great. I smiled at the cars driving by and felt sorry for those who were missing this moment of pure freedom. Many of those people probably thought that I was crazy running in this rain, but I didn't care a bit. For a moment the kid in me took control, and I was stepping in the puddles and mud and laughing at myself. I came home soaked from head to toe but was as happy as can be. In fact this was one of my most enjoyable runs in years. This is what running is all about. Freeing ourselves from all artificial and self imposed limitations and returning to our basic human nature allowing our free spirit to take control, at least for the run.

Whatever stage you are in as a runner the important thing is not to let running become one more routine task of your daily life. Instead let running be the escape from the daily commitments of your life. Run free and enjoy each run. Having said this, sometimes during a run I find myself running on automatic pilot. In other words, my mind is filled with thoughts of daily life and I'm not really conscious of the run especially when I'm familiar with the surrounding area. This is fine but it can take away some of the enjoyment of the run. When the run is over you may not remember anything you saw because your mind was elsewhere. To put my mind more in the run I focus on the details of things along the course. For example a tree, a building, other people, etc. Looking at the immediate surroundings quickly brings me back to the present. This makes me be more aware of each running experience.

Running puts you in touch with your inner self.

# Part Five: *Running*
## *Lifestyle*

---

"And in the end it's not the years in your life that count. It's the life in your years."
(Abraham Lincoln)

# Chapter 11 - Staying Healthy

I believe that the key to a long lasting running experience is to maintain a balanced lifestyle. The human body is a marvelous machine but it needs care just like anything else in the world. We cannot neglect it and expect that it will always perform to meet our demands. Eventually our inconsistent behavior will catch up with us. Many times I have seen people living a life of extremes. On the one hand they push their bodies to the physical limits, while on the other they don't take good care of themselves. They drink too much, overeat, or barely sleep. With this behavior they are cheating themselves. Exercising alone without moderation in other areas of our lives will not do us much good in the long run. To maintain a healthy lifestyle is not difficult but it requires desire, will power and consistency. The following pages contain several common sense ideas that can help you with your running lifestyle. Please keep in mind that I am not a medical expert so this information is not intended to replace any medical or professional advice. Always seek professional advice when in doubt.

## A Runner's Diet

We are a reflection of what we eat. By this I mean that what we put in our stomach has a direct influence on the quality of life we live. As runners our diet is our fuel. It makes sense then that the food we eat be of the type to boost our system and not to break it down. Nowadays there are dozens of books on nutrition and related topics available. My goal here is not to get into a deep nutritional discussion, but to provide some general ideas on what has worked for me as a runner.

I don't believe in dieting alone as a method to lose weight. In most cases these regimens are very difficult to sustain long term and don't provide lasting benefits. This is because the body's metabolism becomes very efficient during the diet, and it is able to get by with significantly fewer calories. As soon as the diet is over and we resume normal eating the body gains weight because it is now receiving more food than it needs. However, most of us can benefit from changes in our diet. We can improve our nutrition by avoiding certain types of food or at least reducing their consumption. Some of the well-known types to avoid are fatty foods especially those with animal fat.

If your goal is to lose weight I believe that the best method is to combine moderate exercise like running with a balanced diet. The advantage of this approach is that it is more effective than dieting alone. When evaluating the foods you eat on a regular basis consider replacing those that don't add much nutritional value to your diet. Usually these are the ones with high fat and sugar content. A balanced diet should consist mainly of grains, vegetables and fruits (carbohydrates). Protein rich foods (meats, fish, legumes) and dairy products are next in importance with fats and sugars to be eaten sparingly. If you are a vegetarian you should still strive for a balanced diet, but replace meats with legumes for protein.

The following are a few tips for runners:

- Many of us have heard the term carbo load. For those who haven't, this is related to eating food that contains lots of carbohydrates prior to a big run or race. Bread, cereal, rice, and pasta are some of the foods rich in carbos. Carbohydrates transform into glycogen, which is the main fuel our muscles use during a run. For best results, start carbo loading two or three days prior to the race and cut down on red meats and foods that take longer to digest.
- Proteins are a necessary component of a healthy diet. Fish is one of the best and leanest sources of the proteins. In fact, regularly consuming moderate amounts of fish may reduce blood pressure and help maintain a healthy heart.

- Don't abuse alcohol. If you drink, moderation is common sense if you expect a long healthy running experience. Avoid alcohol the day before a race.
- As runners we need strong bones. Calcium is essential to maintain healthy bones. Include calcium-rich dairy products in your diet.
- Include a multivitamin in your diet especially for antioxidants and vitamins C & E.
- Most natural juices, especially citrus, are a great source of vitamin C. This vitamin strengthens the immune system, which can be weakened by too much running.
- After two hours of continuous running the glycogen reserves in the muscles are mostly depleted. Sport bars and gels are a great source of fuel energy during this time. They help replenish the glycogen in the muscles. It is best to experiment with this type of concentrated energy food to see how your stomach tolerates it. If this doesn't work try candy or a banana. For best results, drink water or a sports drink with this food.
- Bananas are an excellent source of potassium needed by our working muscles. Eat them anytime but especially after a run.
- Strive for a balanced diet. For example break down your daily calorie intake so that 60% comes from carbohydrates, 25% from fats, and 15% from proteins. For adequate percents for you consult with a nutrition specialist.
- Avoid deep-fried foods and high-fat foods.
- Don't eat less than 1200 calories per day unless prescribed by your doctor. Most weight loss programs recommend that you don't lose more than 1-2 lbs per week.
- When measuring body weight, the total body fat percent is more meaningful than total body weight. In other words, the percent of fat in the body is what must be measured to determine if the person is really overweight. Someone could weigh a lot but have normal body fat percent meaning that they don't need to lose weight.
- It is better to eat many small meals throughout the day instead of three big ones. This allows the body to be more efficient by frequently refueling.

My philosophy is to look for balance in my diet. I try to stay away from high-fat foods. My diet consists mainly of carbohydrates with protein from fish and chicken. I eat lots of vegetables and fruits. I love orange juice and drink a few glasses every day. I drink water all day to stay hydrated for my runs. I don't drink coffee. Instead I drink hot tea a couple of times a day. I seldom drink alcohol except for a glass of wine once in a while. I don't eat much red meat. I take a multivitamin every day. Sometimes I eat a sports bar or gel as a snack prior to running or during a long run over 14 miles. For races my diet doesn't change much except that I increase the carbohydrates and fluids, and decrease the protein intake. After a race I eat several bananas and drink lots of water followed by a healthy meal later on. This is what works for me. My advice is to try out different things until you feel comfortable with a specific diet. If something doesn't work then try something else. Nothing is written in stone. Each year new discoveries and theories about nutrition come out, which proves that this is an evolving subject.

For more information check the references in Appendix-A.

## Staying Hydrated

The human body is over 75% water. We all need water to survive on a day to day basis. As runners staying hydrated is of utmost importance. We cannot afford to get dehydrated and risk our running and our health. Therefore, it is important to always drink plenty of fluids before and after a run. On hot days drink extra water before running and consider bringing water with you especially if going for a long run. By long runs I mean over one hour but in some cases it could be less. Running in the Florida heat you can lose almost 4 lbs of body weight through sweat every hour of running. Don't neglect to replace lost fluids often to prevent dehydration. Thirst is not a good indicator to use since by then you have already started to get dehydrated. My advice is to learn to keep your body hydrated by just drinking lots of fluids all the time. It is better to drink more fluids than needed than not enough and get sick.

When running continuously for over one hour it is better to drink water and a sports drink that contains electrolytes. Electrolytes have sodium and potassium. These are lost through sweat and are needed by your body. When hydrating avoid alcohol and caffeine drinks. These are diuretic and will make you lose more fluids, which is the opposite effect you want. Sodas and natural juices are more likely to upset your stomach because of carbonation or acidity, not a good thing especially right before a race. The most effective fluids are water and sports drinks.

Hopefully, you will never experience dehydration but some signs are thirst, dry mouth, feeling light headed, dizziness, headache, muscle cramps, nausea, fatigue, and dark urine. If you have any of these symptoms while running stop right away and seek help if necessary.

**The Healing Power of Rest**

Rest is necessary for our general well being. Time off is a must for long term healthy running. Sometimes we get stuck in a training schedule and find it difficult to slow down, especially if we believe that we will regress from our current running condition. I know this because I don't like to skip my designated running days, but a few times in my running career I have been forced to cut back for as much as two weeks because of work or family reasons. Other times I had to stop running for a few days because of an injury or a minor illness. Rest will do miracles to help us recover from over training, illness, or just plain burnout. Allowing adequate time to recover is crucial for a long-term successful running career. I believe that if you have been running consistently for a year you can take two weeks off without losing your current shape. In fact, you will feel renewed when you go back to the roads. The time off allows the muscles to rebuild themselves and be stronger for when you return. Every time I was off the road for a few days I felt stronger, lighter, and re-energized when going back. The rest period allowed me to recover and regain power to start again. I believe that it makes sense to include a few rest periods in your running schedule throughout the year. A couple of weeks off every six months may work well for you. Try it out, your body will thank you.

In addition to taking time off from running it is important to get enough sleep on a daily basis, especially while training. Make sure that you get the sleep your body needs. If you find yourself always tired or falling asleep during the day then you are not getting enough hours of sleep. Not all people need the same amount of sleep. It seems that as we get older we require less hours of sleep. My wife and I need eight hours of sleep to feel completely rested the next day, while some older friends feel great with only five or six hours. The number of hours each person needs varies with the individual, but you can find out by checking the number of hours it takes for you to wake up feeling rested. Getting the adequate amount of sleep every night can benefit you in all aspects of your life including your running performance.

## Healthy Running Tips

I am a believer in prevention. Although we can never anticipate all the problems we will encounter we can at least avoid most by using our instinct and common sense. The following are some practical tips to help you make your running experience healthy and long lasting.

- Always listen to your body for signs of potential problems. The body usually gives us warnings when something is not right. A common mistake is to ignore these until they become more serious. Remember that an ounce of prevention is worth a pound of cure. It is far better to lose a few days of running than to get a more serious problem that can keep you off the road much longer. Seek medical advice when in doubt.

- If while running you feel lightheaded, dizzy, or experience chest pain stop immediately. Although not always life threatening these could be signs of a more serious condition. Seek medical help if necessary.

- There is some controversy about running while pregnant. Although some women run during most of their pregnancies without complication you should always consult with your doctor prior to starting or resuming your running.

- There is no absolute proof that running everyday is better for performance than running every other day. I believe that the quality of your runs is more important than the quantity. Running everyday can cause overuse injuries or faster burn out for many people. Leaving a rest day in between runs will allow more time for muscle recovery. By running alternate days you may experience fewer injuries and improve performance.

- The feet are one of the most forgotten parts of the body and yet one of the most essential for our running. Don't neglect this important part of your body. Keep your toenails trimmed to avoid blisters or bruises caused by friction during a run. Rest your feet after a hard day by keeping them elevated. A hot bath and a little cornstarch powder feel great. Your feet deserve a little pampering once in a while.

- Don't hang around in wet, sweaty clothes after a run. The warm, moist environment encourages skin irritation and fungus problems. Shower as soon as possible after running.

## Common Running Aches and Afflictions

The following are some of the most common running related ailments. If you experience any of these for more than a few days consult with your doctor.

- *Side Stitch*: A sharp pain felt in the side below the ribs. This is common among beginners. It can be caused by swallowing too much air without exhaling or by having eaten right before running. For relief take deep breaths using your stomach muscles to relax the area of the stitch. If this doesn't work walk for a few steps while continuing to breathe deeply and trying to relax.

- *Jock Itch*: Typical symptoms are itching and irritation in the groin area. This is mainly a male problem caused by friction and inadequate ventilation of the groin area during and after exercise. The excessive moisture and warmth can encourage the development of fungus when not properly cleaned. To avoid this problem, shower soon after exercise and try to keep the groin area dry. If the itching doesn't go away contact your doctor to get anti-fungal medication.

Unlike the bruises, sprains, and breaks found in other sports, most running afflictions are due to overuse. In other words they are caused by continuous stress applied to an area of the body.

Because running involves mainly the lower part of the body this is where we get most of the injuries.

- *Achilles Tendinitis*: This condition affects the Achilles tendon. The pain is felt around the Achilles area and lower back part of the leg. Some of causes of this problem are increased mileage, overuse, worn out shoes, or tight calf muscles. When this condition occurs make sure to take time off from running. Some icing and stretching may help as well. Seek medical help if the pain persists after a few days. Women should avoid wearing high heels right before running since a sudden switch to running shoes can increase the risk of this ailment by overstretching the tendon.

- *Ankle sprains*: This occurs when the foot rolls inward too far overstretching the ligaments, muscles, or tendons of the ankle. When this happens swelling usually occurs around the affected area. Apply ice to the swollen area and keep the foot elevated. Seek medical help if the pain is too intense or the swelling doesn't go away.

- *Heat exhaustion*: This occurs when the body overheats due to dehydration or running in very high temperatures. In hot climates like Florida runners should take precautions to avoid this problem. Some of the symptoms are dizziness, thirst, headache, disorientation, fatigue, and muscle cramps. In more serious cases there could be nausea, pale skin, and a decrease in sweat rate. If any of these symptoms occur stop running. Drink water or a sports beverage, but drink it slowly. Seek medical help. To avoid heat exhaustion dress lighter, drink plenty of fluids, and don't run during the hottest time of the day.

- *Heel pain*: This is usually known as Plantar Fascitis/ Heel Spur Syndrome because it involves the Plantar Fascia ligament, which extends from the heel to the toes. Overstretching this ligament can cause pain and inflammation in the heel area. Some of the causes of this problem are overuse and using shoes with too little arch support. Rest, ice, and stretching are part of the treatment. If the condition doesn't improve after a few days consult with a professional.

- *Knee pain*: The knee is the most complex joint of the body. Knee problems can affect several areas around the knee. There are many possible causes of knee pain ranging from years of wear and tear to worn out shoes or a genetic predisposition. Because the knee is so complex, if the pain doesn't go away in a few days with rest, icing, and taking an over-the-counter anti-inflammatory get professional help.

- *Lower back pain*: This is common among runners. Pain can be caused several reasons including the strain of supporting the upper body, excessive wear and tear, injuries, or an imbalance between the abdomen and back muscles. The lower back acts as a shock absorber when we run. Every time the feet hit the ground the impact force is propagated through the legs to the lower back muscles which lessen the shock. It is important to strengthen these muscles by doing abs and lower back exercises. If the lower back pain doesn't go away after a few days check with a doctor for proper diagnosis and treatment.

- *Muscle fatigue*: This involves muscle soreness, pain or inflammation after a hard run or race. It could be a symptom of over training or that you are not allowing enough recovery time between workouts. To avoid this stretch after runs, try to get a massage after hard races, and make sure to allow plenty of rest time to allow the glycogen reserves in your muscles to recover. If the condition persists after a few days take more time off and check with a professional if necessary.

- *Shin splints*: This is another common affliction among runners. The pain is usually felt in the shin, the front part of the leg between the foot and the knee. Although there are many causes of shin pain some common ones are running on hard surfaces, worn out shoes, and a muscle imbalance condition between the shin and the calf. If you experience this problem get some rest and look at what may have caused this condition. If the pain doesn't go away within a few days seek medical help.

Obviously this is not a complete list of running related ailments. There are many more potential aches and injuries. The point is that you should always seek professional help when in doubt or if the problem doesn't go away by itself within a few days. After years of running I have come to realize that most injuries runners experience are the result of over-training, lack of adequate stretching, or a muscle imbalance condition. Usually when something goes wrong it is not just a random event but the consequence of our actions. I know that with a little effort on our part we can prevent or minimize many of these troubles. For more information about running related injuries check the references in Appendix-A.

The following is a list of additional tips that may help you deal with potential running problems.

- Joint pain is considered more serious than muscle ache and should be evaluated by a professional.
- If you have an injury involving swelling (i.e. knee pain) avoid hot tubs which can cause more swelling. Instead take a shower and apply ice to the swollen area.
- One of the best ways to prevent injuries is to stretch and strengthen your muscles regularly.
- Muscle imbalance is usually one of the causes of injuries. For example, weak stomach muscles can put more strain on the lower back causing low back pain.
- It is a good idea for runners to always keep an ice pack at home. For best results get a soft ice pack, which will even stay soft in the freezer.
- Running downhill has a higher risk of injuries than running uphill.
- Use common sense if you have any type of running ache. Rest is a great cure. Cut back on your running if necessary.

If you experience a running related injury in some cases you may be able to treat it yourself with rest, ice, compression, and elevation (RICE). This first-aid treatment may not be suitable for serious injuries. Use your judgment, but if this self-treatment doesn't help in a few days get medical help.

Sometimes a good massage can do wonders to relax our tightened muscles especially after a hard race or strenuous workout. There are several types and intensities of massages. If you have never had one you should try it sometime. At most races they offer free massages. A great bargain, but even if you have to pay they are worth it. Last year I got my first complete massage a few days prior to the 15K River Run. This helped me tremendously to loosen up my muscles before the big race.

I believe that our body is very strong and can take a lot of abuse, but it is not invincible. We need to treat it gently and observe prevention to avoid injuries that will keep us away from running. Listen to your body. It is usually right.

So far we have talked about the runner's diet, how to stay healthy, and some common running ailments, but I haven't told you where to go for professional advice. For medical help there are specialized sports physicians as well as sports chiropractors. In Jacksonville, there are many excellent professionals. Check the yellow pages for a complete listing or ask your primary physician for references. Another option is to call some of the local hospitals for referrals. Probably the best option is to ask other runners for referrals since they may already know someone they trust.

The same goes for sports nutritionists. If you need their professional advice you can find these people in the phone book or through referrals. Call the local hospitals for information or ask your sports doctor for a referral. Additionally, some fitness clubs have qualified nutritional staff available.

**Stress Reduction Tips**

Do you ever feel stressed out or like there is no light at the end of the tunnel? If the answer is yes you are not alone. In today's fast paced world, stress is becoming more and more common. The following are some indicators of stress.

- Cannot sleep well. Sleeping less than 5 hours per night.
- Difficulty getting out of bed in the morning.
- Loss of appetite. Sometimes the opposite, overeating.
- Loss of energy. Often feeling tired or burned out.
- Worrying too much. Everything makes you nervous or tense.
- Difficulty making decisions.
- Difficulty concentrating. Have lost interest in most things.
- A pessimistic or negative attitude about everything.

- Spending more time sad than happy.
- Low self-esteem. Not feeling good about self.
- Never have time for leisure activities. Cannot relax.
- Frequent digestive problems.
- An unexplained loss or gain of several pounds.

If you have more than one of the above symptoms you may be experiencing some level of stress. The good news is that there are simple ways to reduce stress or at least keep it under control. One of the most effective ways you already know, which is to exercise or run, but there are several more things you can do as well.

If you feel that the stress symptoms are very strong and cannot cope with them you may be experiencing depression or anxiety. For these conditions it is best to seek professional help from your doctor.

The following are some stress relieving activities.

- Exercise regularly. Go for a run. Stretch.
- Do more leisure activities. Read books, listen to music, play with your kids, watch movies, take walks, learn to play an instrument, etc.
- Schedule in leisure activities just as you do work activities.
- Take a hot bath once a week.
- Practice a form of relaxation such as yoga, meditation, or Tai-chi. For example, take 5 minutes each day to relax and meditate about the events of the day. Do this sitting in a quiet area. The day has 1440 minutes so no matter how busy you are 5 minutes is doable. Try it, you will enjoy it.
- Cut the number of daily activities you do in half.
- Think of the good things you have in your life.
- Think of how many people are less fortunate than you are.
- Laugh often.
- Put things in perspective. Think if your worries will matter in a year from now.
- Talk to a friend or seek professional advice.

These are just a few of many things you can do to reduce the stress in your life. The point is that we don't have to take life so seriously. Everyone has bad days. We can make a mountain out of every negative event or we can see the positive in every experience and move on. It is our choice every time.

A lot of times we make ourselves miserable by trying to do too many tasks at the same time. We set unrealistic expectations as if this were the last day of our lives. The truth is that most tasks could be forgotten and our lives would not be affected at all. In fact life may improve due to the benefit of having more time to relax. Next time you feel overwhelmed by the number of things you are trying to do, cut them in half. This is a good rule to remember. Believe me, the world will not come to a stop, and you will be a lot happier with less weight on your shoulders. Simple is better. From now on make it a point to simplify your life a little. In my experience, the greatest moments are usually the simplest.

# Chapter 12  - Family Running

Running is a great family activity. This is because running blends well with family life. All ages and abilities are welcome and celebrated at running events making this the perfect family activity that can span generations. The simplicity and openness of running invites everyone to share the experience either as active participants or enthusiastic observers. Running gives us the opportunity to spend time together with our families while doing something healthy and fun, a win-win situation for everybody.

## Running with Kids

Running with your kids can be a very special experience. It can give you an activity in common that can last a lifetime. What better way to stay close with your son or daughter? It will strengthen your relationship with them. You will forever cherish the runs together.

There is no doubt in my mind that running sets a very positive and healthy example for kids. As runners we become role models for other people but especially for our children. When I started running my kids were very small so they couldn't take much part in this experience, but as they got older I started asking them to run with me and bringing them to races.

From experience I know that sometimes it can be difficult to get kids started in running. They may refuse or give you many excuses. After all it takes a lot of physical effort to run more than a block, but once they have done it a few times kids will usually want to run again. So the goal is to get them to run or walk a few times to build their self-confidence. There are many ways to motivate your kids to run. The first time I asked my daughter to run she didn't want to. I had to work hard to convince her that it would be fun for her. After the first few times she started to enjoy it. With my son it was a lot easier. He wanted to run. I guess he wanted to be like me. Trying to keep my daughter motivated I asked her to come along on my training runs. Since she couldn't keep up with my pace she rode her bike or roller bladed next to me. These were great father and daughter times together. After a while she was asking me when we would go out again. Another thing I did with my kids was to tell them running was a game. I told them that it was fun to run with other kids and to be able to complete the mile. Other times I offered them a reward like buying them a book of their choice or taking them to the movies. This was not bribery but a way to reward good practices. Eventually kids will learn to like running because of its intrinsic rewards and not because they can get something material. Some children are naturally more competitive than others, so they need to feel like they are winning something. This is what keeps them motivated. Other kids don't need convincing. They just like running and want to do it every time. Either way you need to use your imagination to get them started.

Although the purpose of this section is not to provide professional advice for children in sports there are a few common sense points that should be considered:

- Before engaging in any exercise activity with your kids, obtain their primary physician's approval. A medical evaluation is always recommended prior to starting an intensive aerobic sport such as running. Make sure to tell the doctor the types of activities you plan to do with them.

- Depending on the kids' age and natural ability you should set attainable goals for their running. This will only encourage them to continue running when they reach those goals.

- Never force young kids to run against their will. This will only create a negative effect, which could make them reject sports later in life. You should only make suggestions by presenting this as something fun and good for them. Always let them have the final word on running or not.

- When running with your kids be patient with them. Many times I have seen parents trying to do a good thing the wrong way. Show your kids that you care by being gentle in the way you teach them. It breaks my heart to see kids being scolded for no other reason that not playing the sport the way their parents wished they did. Put things into perspective. Sports are supposed to be fun, not punishment. Yelling at kids for every mistake they make will only make them more insecure for years to come. Instead of pointing out their mistakes all the time tell them how much they have progressed and how proud you are of them. Do it with love. In the long run the quality of the experience is much more important than whether they get to be champions or not. Make the running experience a positive time for you and your kids. They will always cherish this time spent with you. I know that sometimes it is hard to control our winning instincts, but let's not try to live our own unfulfilled dreams through our kids. Let them be themselves.

- When kids start running for the first time there should be a slow progression. Don't expect them to do as much as you especially if they are under 10 years old. Start by combining walking and jogging for short distances. Slowly increase to jogging and running. Use your judgment to evaluate their readiness to run farther or go faster. If the child wants to stop let him/her do it. There is no shame in walking the entire distance. Always take into account their age and physical limitations.

- Kids tend to overheat faster than average adults. This is especially important in the high heat months since kids can overheat to dangerous levels. For very young kids it is better to avoid running in the summer months. Instead try cooler activities like water sports.

- Don't forget to praise your kids often. Running is no small effort, and in a big way they are running to please you. Be proud of them and let them know it.

- Running with kids should be fun. This is the best way to keep them motivated for a long time.

When training with your kids decide what distances they will run. If they are very young don't make them run the same as you. They couldn't keep up in most cases. Running road distances takes a lot of physical effort, and it is very different than running on the track. I believe most kids under 10 should not run more than a mile or two. When I run with my kids we go for a half-mile loop that I know they can finish. Since they only enter fun runs we start training a couple of weeks before each event. This is plenty of running for them.

**Family Fun Run**

The fun run is a 1-mile or shorter race for kids and their families. Many road races have a fun run after the main event. Although many fun runs are free some require a small fee but this usually includes a tee-shirt. Most fun runs require participants to fill out an entry form.

The fun run is a very nice way to get young kids started in running. The distance can seem a lot for someone that has never run before, but it is doable with a little training. Kids can run and walk if they wish. The main goal is to have fun while getting kids involved in a healthy sport. At most fun runs finishers get a ribbon. This helps them remember their accomplishment and feel proud about it. When my daughter was 6 years old, she ran her first 1-mile race with my wife. She felt very proud of her accomplishment. Since then she has been running several fun runs every year. My son ran his first fun run at age 5, the Junior River Run mile. My daughter and I ran with him that day and he beat both of us. That morning my wife and I had run the 15K River Run, so this was the first time that the whole family had run a race on the same day.

I believe that the fun run gives parents a great opportunity to get their kids involved in running. Besides it is fun to run with your children while they are still young. I bet that they will always remember those special moments with you. Next time you are planning to enter a race see if they have a fun run. It may be a chance for the whole family to run together.

**Running with your Partner**

Running can be an excellent activity to do together with your spouse or significant other. It can make the relationship a lot richer since you will have something both can enjoy and talk about. If you are used to running alone think if it wouldn't be more fun to combine some of those lonely runs with your partner. So next time invite him/her to run with you. If this is their first run tell them that walking is okay. Eventually they will get better. Regardless of differences in your running abilities this can be a very positive experience for you both. A few runs together every month will go a long way to spark a relationship. With a little imagination you can plan running dates with your partner combining training and races together in different locations. After running for several years I finally convinced my wife to start running. She got motivated by running the fun runs with our kids and seeing the positive effects running had on me. One day she told me that she wanted to run a 5K. I helped her with a training plan and encouraged her to keep working towards her running goals. Although we trained at different paces we did several runs together. A few months ago we left our kids with my in-laws and went for a morning run at Doctors Lake park in Orange Park. The shaded trail and smooth slopes made for a very romantic setting for our run. After the run we headed to the nearest coffee shop for bagels and hot beverages. Doing our runs together makes our running a lot more interesting. Plus it gives us a reason to get out of the house and do something unusual. Another run that we like to do is at the beach in the evening. Running together by the ocean is very romantic. In addition you should plan races together so that you have a common goal ahead. Since my wife started running we have done several races together. Although we run the race at different speeds we share the excitement of the start and celebrate together at the finish.

Because running is also an individual activity I am not advocating that you always run together. That is your choice, but when you do run together it is important to keep things in perspective. The relationship should always be first over running. Avoid getting too competitive with each other. Use running as an activity to bring you closer and not to set you apart. The point is that with a little planning and mutual desire you can make running a positive aspect of your relationship with your partner. Together you can share each other's progress, plan for running activities, and be proud of your accomplishments.

I believe that the best way to get family members involved in running is to bring them along to races and other running activities. The excitement at these events is contagious, and the more they see you running the more they may want to try it out for themselves. Basically, all it takes is your encouragement and their willingness to try. One of my favorite activities is to sign up for a race out-of-town and bring the family along. This turns into a small vacation for everyone. One of our future running projects with my wife is to go on a running vacation just the two of us. But we'll have to wait until our kids are a little older.

Running makes me very happy, but being able to share my running experiences with my family makes me even happier.

**Running with your Dog**

Dogs love to run around. It is in their nature. If you have an active dog you may have a potential running companion. Although most dogs can run, some breeds are more suited than others for this type of exercise. To avoid problems consult with the dog's vet before making your friendly pet run with you.

When you first start running with a dog it should be a slow progression from walking to jogging and then running. Don't assume that the dog can run as much as you the first time. Dogs need to develop their stamina too. Eventually you will be catching up with him, but start slow and build up to the desired distance.

Our three-year old mixed Lab and German Shepherd has become my family's loyal and always ready running partner. My wife started taking her on runs when she was about one year old. The dog loved running and became very good in a short time. In fact, my wife couldn't keep up with her after a few weeks. By this time my wife was asking me to take her on my runs. Initially I refused

180

since I thought the dog would be more of a nuisance than a loyal companion, but the family insisted and soon after I was taking the dog in some of my runs. At first it required a little bit of adjustment on my part since I had to make a few stops to let the dog sniff something on the road, but eventually I started to feel very relaxed with my new friend. Now I always take her on my night runs. My wife takes her on some of her morning runs. This way she gets plenty of exercise. Running is the big event of the day for her. As soon as she sees my running shoes she knows we are going for a run. She starts barking and her whole face transforms when we open the gate to get out of the yard. She loves to run and doesn't seem to ever get tired. Actually, we have to keep up with her. Sometimes on our night runs I let her loose, and she runs back and forth checking the surroundings but making sure to keep me within sight. One of her favorite tricks is to find a ditch with a few inches of water and sprint up and down splashing water and mud all over herself. It is just great to watch her. One time she stayed behind and lost sight of my wife. When she realized that she was alone she traced her way back to the house, arriving before my wife did.

Running with your dog can be a fun experience and time well spent. The dog loves to be with you and to get out of the house. This way the dog is happy and gets exercise, you get your running, and you will feel good doing a good deed for your canine friend. Additionally, if you run at night or in isolated areas taking the dog with you can be a big deterrent to anyone with bad intentions.

If you plan to run with your dog in public areas a few rules should be observed to make yours and others' runs safe and fun.

- If you run in an area with lots of people or where there is traffic keep the dog on a leash. Although you may know that your dog is friendly, others will feel intimidated by the presence of a loose dog especially if it is a big animal.
- It is a good idea to start training your dog to run when the dog is relatively young preferably before two years of age.
- Learn to detect early signs of exhaustion in your dog. Dogs don't sweat like humans. If the dog slows down or refuses to continue, stop running and let the dog walk for a while. Always give the dog plenty of fresh water after the run.

For all running dogs and their owners Jacksonville has a 5K Dog race every year. This unique event is held around the middle of September. If you have been running with your dog this is a great opportunity to share the excitement of a race with your loyal friend. The race is held early in the morning on the beach. Proceeds from the run benefit the local humane society. In 1998 my wife and daughter ran this race with our dog. It was an unbelievable sight to see hundreds of dogs and their owners running together. Dogs and people were having a great time. After the race there were treats for both the human and canine athletes.

The fun run, a great event for kids and grown ups alike.

Running, a sport for the whole family.

A dog can be a loyal running companion.

# Epilogue

Now that you have read the book, I hope that you have enjoyed reading it as much as I enjoyed writing it.

When I first got the idea to write a book four years ago, my main goal was to share my running experiences so that perhaps others would benefit from this information. Basically, I wanted to provide the insight and common sense tips about running that I was looking for when I first started and couldn't find in one bundle. My purpose will have been met if I was able to contribute in any way to make your running experience more enjoyable and safe.

If there is one message I want to leave you with, it is that the real joy of running is not to add more miles or break more PRs, but just to be able to run. Three weeks ago I was reminded of this when an unexpected flu ruined my plan to run the traditional Thanksgiving half marathon. After a long week without running, I entered a local 5K race for charity. Being back on the road was the greatest gift I could have asked for. I thanked God for my good fortune.

Best of luck, friends. See you out on the roads.

# APPENDIX A – Useful References

When I started running the roads I didn't know much about the world of runners. I was hungry for information and answers to my questions but didn't know where to go. As in everything worth pursuing in life, it takes time and patience to learn about the things you want. With this thought in mind I have collected the following running references throughout the years. This is by no means a complete list, but should be a good start especially for someone new to running.

The information has been divided into local and general references. If you wish to find out more running information one of the best tools to use today is the internet. This is like having access to a worldwide up-to-date encyclopedia from the convenience of your home. Use this vast resource to look for the information you need. In most cases you will find what you are looking for. For those that don't have access to the internet many local libraries have computers available for this use.

<u>Note</u>: Although the author has made an extraordinary effort to give accurate information, the author assumes no responsibility whatsoever. The information provided below is subject to change without notice.

**Local References**

<u>Running Stores</u>

*1ˢᵗ Place Sports* (<u>www.1stplacesports.com</u>): Owned by Doug and Jane Alred, this running only store has been in business since the late 70s. Throughout all these years 1ˢᵗ Place Sports has been at the forefront of the running community in Jacksonville. Besides having one of the most complete lines of running and walking equipment in the area this store has become a center of local running information for Jacksonville. The staff is very knowledgeable and friendly. The store has two locations: 3853 Baymeadows Road in Jacksonville (904) 731-3676 and at the Sawgrass Village in Ponte Vedra Beach (904) 280-3007.

*FunRun Sports* (www.fun-run.com): Owned by Chris Martoglio, this is St. Augustine's leading fitness store specializing mainly in running, walking, and swimming gear. The staff is very friendly and knowledgeable. Join them at the store every Saturday and Sunday at 7:30am for FunRun Community Group Run & Walk. FunRun Sports is located at 1073 A1A Beach Boulevard in St. Augustine Beach. The phone number is (904) 460-4848.

Running Clubs

*Jacksonville Track Club (JTC)*: Started in the 70s, this is one of the oldest and largest running clubs in Northeast Florida. The club is open to all runners and walkers. The JTC hosts several races every year including the world famous River Run 15K. The club is a member of the RRCA and USATF. The club publishes a monthly newsletter, The Starting Line. An annual membership fee is required. For more information call (904) 384-8725, or write to JTC, P.O. Box 24667, Jacksonville, FL 32241. The JTC's web site is (www.jacksonvilletrackclub.com).

*Florida Striders Track Club*: Based in Orange Park, the club is over twenty years old. The Striders club is open to all runners, walkers and their families. They are very organized and family oriented. Several running and social activities are held every month. The Striders host four well-known races every year including the traditional Autumn Fitness 5K and the Memorial Day 5K. The club publishes a monthly newsletter, Strideright. The Striders club is a member of the RRCA and USATF. An annual membership fee is required. For more information write to Florida Striders, P.O. Box 413, Orange Park, FL 32067-0413.

*1st Place Sports Running Club*: Started in 1996, this is a very competitive running team. The club is a member of the RRCA and

USATF. The club hosts over 20 well-known road races every year including the Jacksonville Marathon and the Run for the Pies 5K. The Jacksonville Running News is published by 1st Place Sports every quarter. A membership fee is required. For more information contact 1st Place Sports at (904) 731-3676 or check their web site at (www.1stplacesports.com).

*Ancient City Road Runners (ACRR)*: Based in St. Augustine, this running club is open to runners of all ages and abilities. The ACRR hosts several races and social events throughout the year including the well-known Matanzas 5K. A membership fee is required. The club is a member of the RRCA and USATF organizations. For more information check their web site at (http://members.aol.com/acrrclub) or write to ACRR, P.O. Box 4111, St. Augustine, FL, 32085-4111.

*Beach Endurance Sports Team (BEST)*: Based in the beaches area, this is a group of fitness oriented people including runners, cyclists, swimmers and walkers. The club is open to anyone wanting to participate in the fitness and social activities available. The club hosts several race events every year. A membership fee is required. For more information contact Performance MultiSports at (904) 285-1552 or check their web site (http://users.ilnk.com/Performance).

*Hash House Harriers (HHH)*: Although the HHH are an international organization, Jacksonville has local representation of this alternative approach to running. For more information call (904) 247-4875 or check their web site at (http://www.jacksonville.net/~jaxhashes). The national web site is (http://www.harrier.org).

*Florida Track Club (FTC)*: Based in Gainesville, this is a very active running club. It is open to runners of all ages and abilities. The club hosts several races, fun runs, and social events every year. A membership fee is required. The FTC is a member of the RRCA and USATF. For more information call (352) 378-TRAK or write to FTC, P.O. Box 12463, Gainesville, FL 32604. Their web site is (http://www.afn.org/~ftc).

## General Running References

There are literally dozens of running information resources available. These include books, magazines, product reviews, newsletters, and race calendars to name a few. With the introduction of the worldwide web there has been a huge increase in the number of these resources. Today you can find almost every imaginable publication about running on the Internet. Every month new running related sites appear on the worldwide web. This is a great benefit for runners since now we don't have to leave our homes to get access to running advice, race schedules, product information, book reviews, and running magazines. Because the worldwide web is a dynamic resource, the information available is constantly changing. This means that internet sites can move or disappear without notice, but don't despair since due to the vast amount of information available you can always find a useful alternative site.

The following is a list of several running related sites I have found very useful. Please keep in mind that these can move or disappear at anytime.

*Road Runners Club of America (RRCA)*: This is a national organization representing hundreds of road running clubs in the United States. Their web site (http://www.rrca.org) contains lots of useful information including the list and contact names of all the registered running clubs. The RRCA publishes a quarterly newsletter, Foot Notes.

*United States Track and Field (USATF)*: This organization is the governing body for track and field in the United States. Their web site (http://www.usatf.org) has the latest official running news and useful information for both track and road running.

*Dr. Pribut's Running Injuries Page*: This is a very useful reference site with lots of injury related information. The web site is (http://www.clark.net/pub/pribut/spsport.html).

*HealthGate*: Although not specifically for running this is a very complete site with lots of health related information. The web site is (http://www.healthgate.com).

*Florida Calendar*: This is a race calendar maintained by Alta Vista Sports. Their web site is (http://www.cuattheraces.com).

*Florida Running & Triathlon*: This is a race calendar publication for Florida. The race schedule can be accessed via their web site at (http://www.runningnetwork.com/members/florida).

*Running Journal*: This is a race calendar publication for the Southeast. The race schedules can be accessed via their web site at (www.RunningNetwork.com/RunningJournal).

*Road Runner Sports*: This is an online running store. It has lots of products and information. Their web site is (http://www.roadrunnersports.com).

*The Track Shack*: This is a running store in Orlando. In addition to a very complete line of running gear it has lots of information for running in Central Florida. Their web site is (http://www.trackshack.com).

*American Running Association*: This is a very complete site with a large variety of running articles and information. Their web site is (http://www.americanrunning.org).

*Cool Running*: This web site (http://www.coolrunning.com) has lots of running advice, useful information, and great links.

*I-Run*: This web site (http://www.i-run.com) has a lot of information for helping you track your miles. If you are a runner who uses a running log check this one out.

*Kick*: This web site (http://www.kicksports.com) offers lots of running advice including sports nutrition and other useful information.

*On the Run*: This is web site (http://www.ontherun.com) contains all sorts of running information and links.

*Running Network*: This web site (http://www.runningnetwork.com) is an excellent resource for race schedules and running information from around the country. Information is grouped by state.

*Running Tips*: This web site (http://www.runningtips.com) offers running tips, training secrets, and product information.

*Runner's Web*: This Canadian web site (http://www.runnersweb.com) has a huge amount of running news, race schedules, interviews, and useful links. This is a very popular running site.

*Running Online*: This web site (http://www.runningonline.com) has lots of running links. Some of these include clubs, races, publications, and training.

*Run the Planet*: This web site (http://www.runtheplanet.com) contains useful information about running in most cities around the world. Check it out if you are planning to go overseas.

*New York Road Runners Club (NYRRC)*: This is a very complete site with lots of information for running in the New York area. If you are planning to enter the New York City Marathon this is the place to get information. Their web site (http://www.nyrrc.org) has great running links including a very complete list of worldwide race schedules.

*Ironman Triathlon*: If you ever thought of doing a triathlon check this cool site (http://www.ironmanlive.com).

*Runner's World*: This is a monthly running magazine available at most bookstores and newsstands. In addition Runner's World offers a great free online version of the magazine with lots of very useful running information covering a broad range of related topics. Some of these include injury prevention, training tips, nationwide race schedules, and running advice. Their web site is located at (http://www.runnersworld.com). This definitely worth checking.

*Running Times*: This is a monthly running magazine available at most bookstores and newsstands. No web site was found for this publication.

*Youth Runner*: This is a quarterly running magazine oriented to kids. It contains useful references to running events for young runners. Their web site is located at (www.youthrunner.com).

**A Few Good Running Books**

The following is a list of a few very informative and inspiring running books I have found. For more titles visit your local bookstore or check the web. Four powerful book search sites are Amazon (http://www.amazon.com); Barnes & Noble (http://www.barnesandnoble.com); Books-A-Million (http://www.booksamillion.com); and Borders at (http://www.borders.com).

*"Better Runs"* by Joe Henderson. 1996, Human Kinetics.

*"Galloway's Book On Running"* by Jeff Galloway. 1984, Shelter Publications, Inc.

*"George Sheehan On Running to Win"* by Dr. George Sheehan. 1994, Rodale Press Inc.

*"Nancy Clark's Sports Nutrition Guidebook"* by Nancy Clark. 1997, Human Kinetics.

*"Healthy Runner's Handbook"* by Lyle Micheli. 1996, Human Kinetics.

*"Marathon: The Ultimate Training Guide"* by Hal Higdon. 1999, Rodale Press Inc.

*"On the Run"* by Grete Waitz. 1997, Rodale Press Inc.

*"PRE America's Greatest Running Legend"* by Tom Jordan. 1997, Rodale Press Inc.

*"Running Injury-Free"* by Joe Ellis and Joe Henderson. 1994, Rodale Press Inc.

*"Ten Million Steps"* by Paul Reese. 1997, Cedarwinds Publishing Company.

*"The Complete Book of Running for Women"* by Claire Kowalchik. 1999, Simon & Schuster.

*"The Ultimate Sports Nutrition Handbook"* by Ellen Coleman. 1996, Bull Publishing Company.

**Running Movies**

The following is a small but selective group of five very good movies about running. I find each film inspiring and unique. These are the types of movies that I never get tired of watching. Perhaps I see myself represented in parts of each of them. Although not always easy to find, I believe all of these films are available in video.

- *"Chariots of Fire" (1981)*: This classic film shows the inspiring story of two great British runners and their journey to the 1924 Olympic games, Eric Lidell and Harold Abrahams.

- *"Running Brave" (1983)*: This film depicts the remarkable story of Billy Mills, a young Native American runner living on a reservation, who through self-determination went on to win the 10,000 meters in the 1964 Olympic games.

- *"Prefontaine" (1997)*: This film recounts the life and running career of legendary runner, Steve Prefontaine.

- *"Without Limits" (1998)*: This is a newer inspirational version of Steve Prefontaine's extraordinary life and running career that were tragically ended in 1975.

- *"Endurance" (1999)*: This unusual film portrays the life of running legend Haile Gebrselassie considered by many to be the greatest long distance runner of all time.

# ~NDIX B – Pace Chart

| Minutes / Mile | 5 km | 5 miles | 10 km | 15 km | Half Marathon | Marathon |
|---|---|---|---|---|---|---|
| 5:00 | 15:32 | 25:00 | 31:04 | 46:36 | 1:05:33 | 2:11:06 |
| 5:15 | 16:19 | 26:15 | 32:37 | 48:56 | 1:08:49 | 2:17:39 |
| 5:30 | 17:05 | 27:30 | 34:11 | 51:16 | 1:12:06 | 2:24:12 |
| 5:45 | 17:52 | 28:45 | 35:44 | 53:36 | 1:15:23 | 2:30:45 |
| 6:00 | 18:38 | 30:00 | 37:17 | 55:55 | 1:18:39 | 2:37:19 |
| 6:15 | 19:25 | 31:15 | 38:50 | 58:15 | 1:21:56 | 2:43:52 |
| 6:30 | 20:12 | 32:30 | 40:23 | 1:00:35 | 1:25:13 | 2:50:25 |
| 6:45 | 20:58 | 33:45 | 41:57 | 1:02:55 | 1:28:29 | 2:56:59 |
| 7:00 | 21:45 | 35:00 | 43:30 | 1:05:15 | 1:31:46 | 3:03:32 |
| 7:15 | 22:31 | 36:15 | 45:03 | 1:07:34 | 1:35:03 | 3:10:05 |
| 7:30 | 23:18 | 37:30 | 46:36 | 1:09:54 | 1:38:19 | 3:16:38 |
| 7:45 | 24:05 | 38:45 | 48:09 | 1:12:14 | 1:41:36 | 3:23:12 |
| 8:00 | 24:51 | 40:00 | 49:43 | 1:14:34 | 1:44:53 | 3:29:45 |
| 8:15 | 25:38 | 41:15 | 51:16 | 1:16:54 | 1:48:09 | 3:36:18 |
| 8:30 | 26:24 | 42:30 | 52:49 | 1:19:13 | 1:51:26 | 3:42:52 |
| 8:45 | 27:11 | 43:45 | 54:22 | 1:21:33 | 1:54:42 | 3:49:25 |
| 9:00 | 27:58 | 45:00 | 55:55 | 1:23:53 | 1:57:59 | 3:55:58 |
| 9:15 | 28:44 | 46:15 | 57:29 | 1:26:13 | 2:01:16 | 4:02:31 |
| 9:30 | 29:31 | 47:30 | 59:02 | 1:28:33 | 2:04:32 | 4:09:05 |
| 9:45 | 30:18 | 48:45 | 1:00:35 | 1:30:53 | 2:07:49 | 4:15:38 |
| 10:00 | 31:04 | 50:00 | 1:02:08 | 1:33:12 | 2:11:06 | 4:22:11 |
| 10:15 | 31:51 | 51:15 | 1:03:42 | 1:35:32 | 2:14:22 | 4:28:45 |
| 10:30 | 32:37 | 52:30 | 1:05:15 | 1:37:52 | 2:17:39 | 4:35:18 |
| 10:45 | 33:24 | 53:45 | 1:06:48 | 1:40:12 | 2:20:55 | 4:41:51 |
| 11:00 | 34:11 | 55:00 | 1:08:21 | 1:42:32 | 2:24:12 | 4:48:24 |
| 11:15 | 34:57 | 56:15 | 1:09:54 | 1:44:52 | 2:27:28 | 4:54:58 |
| 11:30 | 35:44 | 57:30 | 1:11:27 | 1:47:11 | 2:30:45 | 5:01:31 |
| 11:45 | 36:30 | 58:45 | 1:13:01 | 1:49:31 | 2:34:02 | 5:08:04 |
| 12:00 | 37:17 | 1:00:00 | 1:14:34 | 1:51:51 | 2:37:19 | 5:14:37 |
| 12:15 | 38:04 | 1:01:15 | 1:16:07 | 1:54:11 | 2:40:35 | 5:21:11 |
| 12:30 | 38:50 | 1:02:30 | 1:17:40 | 1:56:31 | 2:43:52 | 5:27:44 |

## Conversions

5 km            = 3.107 miles
10 km           = 6.214 miles
15 km           = 9.321 miles
Half Marathon   = 13.109 miles
Marathon        = 26.219 miles

# Order Form

**To order additional copies, fill out this form
and send it along with your check or money
order to: Mauricio Herreros, P.O. Box
600563, Jacksonville, FL 32260-0563**

**Cost per copy $11.95 + $2.00 P&H.  Add
6% State sales tax if mailed to a FL address**

**Ship _____ copies of *Simply Running* to:**

**Name_____**

**Address:_____**

**Address:_____**

**City, State, Zip:_____**

❏     **Check box for signed copy**